THE HARD LIFE

MICHAEL ADAMS

The Hard Life

Religion for Young Adults

with illustrations by Bernard Carr

FOUR COURTS PRESS

The typesetting for this book, in Plantin,
was input by Gilbert Gough Typesetting, Dublin
and output by Printset & Design Ltd, Dublin
for Four Courts Press, Kill Lane, Blackrock, Co. Dublin.

Nihil obstat: Stephen J. Greene, censor deputatus.
Imprimi potest: + Joseph A. Carroll, Administrator, 10 August 1987
(The Nihil Obstat and Imprimi potest are a declaration
that a book or publication is considered
to be free from doctrinal or moral error.
This declaration does not imply approval of,
or agreement with, the contents,
opinions or statements expressed).

© Michael Adams 1987

ACKNOWLEDGEMENT

Quotations from the Bible are for the most part
taken from *The Jerusalem Bible* by permission of the publishers,
Darton, Longman & Todd, London.

First edition Dublin 1977
Second edition Huntingdon, Ind. 1978
Third edition Dublin 1987

BRITISH LIBRARY CATALOGUING IN PUBLICATION DATA

Adams, Michael
The hard life: religion for young adults. — 3rd ed.
1.Christian life — Catholic authors 2.Youth — Religious life
I. Title
248.8'3   BX2355

ISBN 1-85182-018-3

Printed and bound by
The Guernsey Press Co. Ltd., Guernsey, Channel Islands.

For Julian and Gretchen

Contents

Foreword 7
About believing 10
The same old story 23
The four horsemen of the Apocalypse:
   war, pain, hunger, violence 39
Introduction to the hard life 49
Here and now 62
The Catholic standard 75
A sense of identity 85
Notes 94
For further reading 95

Foreword

'Then he said to him a third time, "Simon son of John, do you love me?" Peter was upset that he asked him the third time, "Do you love me", and said, "Lord, you know all things, you know that I love you"' (Jn 21:17).

'When I made you a present of that Life of Christ, I wrote as an inscription: May you seek Christ: may you find Christ: may you love Christ.

'Three perfectly clear stages. Have you tried, at least, to live the first?' (The Way, 382).[1]

Simon Peter was a man who went through those three stages, one after another, reaching the last one only after a painful and humiliating experience. Just imagine a tough brawny fisherman denying his best friend when a slip of a girl calls his bluff. Still, he got there. That's what counts in the end. He came to love Jesus Christ as Jesus Christ wants to be loved; and he proved his love by his actions — as we would like to do.

This book is for those who, like Simon Peter, want to seek, to find and to love Christ. Or at least for those who want to start out on the road.

The fact that you are flicking through the pages of this book in a bookshop (wondering whether to buy or not, wondering whether it's worth the money), or in a library (wondering whether to borrow), or perhaps sitting quietly at home, settled into a comfortable chair (mind you, not *too* comfortable, the author will suggest), ready for a good read — this is proof enough that you have set out on the first stage.

We seek Christ because we sense there is something different about him. We seek Christ because no man has changed or challenged the world quite like he has. We seek Christ because it is not every day of the week that someone dies on a cross for us, 'while we were still sinners' (Rom 5:8). We seek Christ because we know he died and rose again, and lives. And because he lives we must make a choice: either for him or against him.

But where can we find him? In the Church; in Scripture and Tradition; in doctrine, in his sacraments, in his laws; in prayer and sacrifice.

There is nothing sadder than to see a Catholic, who knows by divine faith where God is to be found and yet seeks him where he isn't:

— in paganism instead of in the Church;

— in the thoughts of a so-called revolutionary instead of in sacred Scripture;

— in myths and fables instead of in doctrine;

— in magic, psychotherapy and mass hysteria instead of in the sacraments;

— in human proclamations ('God is dead' and 'all is matter') instead of in God's laws;

— in a selfish monologue with ego instead of in a dialogue of prayer;

— in easygoing self-indulgence instead of in sacrifice.

Having found him we must stay with him by following the way he is going, by living like him. (If we ever cease to live as we ought, we lose him.) And this living is the 'hard life'.

But not as hard as might seem at first sight, for God gives himself to those who give themselves. 'The nearer you go to God, the nearer he will come to you' (Jas 4:8).

He wants to make it easy, as easy as he made it for the two despondent disciples on the road to Emmaus, and for Thomas to whom he offered the sight of his pierced hands and feet and side.

Having found him, go close, go closer still, and you cannot but fall in love with him, and his blessed Mother.

'And what is the secret of perseverance? Love. Fall in love and you will never leave him' (*The Way*, 999).

Charles Connolly

About believing

COMMON SENSE
is common sense, a useful commodity, often in surprisingly short supply.

PHILOSOPHY
is an effort to apply your human mind to your experience. It aims at improving your understanding of life. However 'anti-intellectual' a particular philosophy may be, in its core it is man asking himself 'Why?' If you are a budding Plato or Wittgenstein, you stand a better chance than most of making your own philosophy. If you are a more average kind of person you can learn from other people — and they can teach you. Philosophy, then, is not likely to be the product of arguing with teachers or fellow students: you will be well-advised to *study* if you want to learn philosophy (not everyone does want to: most people do more practical things like mining, or medicine, or looking for a job).

RELIGION
often involves philosophy to some extent but it is less cerebral, less predominantly intellectual. Natural religion consists of various attempts by man to worship, appease and contact the mysteries he senses to exist beneath the surface of life. It expresses itself in prayers, rituals, sacrifices, songs. There is no evidence that religion is to be found only in primitive societies. It is rampant in most societies, although in some places the official philosophy or ideology tries to suppress signs of religion on the grounds that it distracts people's attention from the demands of everyday life — the demands established by the ideologists.

CHRISTIANITY

is not an ideology (a system of ideas, like Marxism or existentialism) which would claim to provide a way for mankind or individuals to get the most out of life. Neither is it a natural religion, a more or less successful attempt to use more than the mind to reach more than the world. The religion of the Church to which Catholics 'belong' is by its own admission a 'supernatural' religion, the outcome of God's personal intervention in human history. The Church professes to have a hold on mysteries or truths taught by God and revealed by his messengers — especially by one messenger, Jesus Christ, who is *the* metaphysical Son of God. He lived, worked, died and rose from the dead, reconciling an estranged mankind to God. The Church tells each generation these truths (which do not change) and offers to believers the means of 'putting on the Lord Jesus Christ' (cf. Rom 13:14). Through these means (mainly preaching and the sacraments) a man, despite his defects, can become like God. Christianity is a special involvement by God in men's affairs, and an involvement by men in God's, by way of response.

RELIGION CLASSES AT SCHOOL

This is the real stuff of religious education. For most people formal religious education stops dead when they finish high school: after that they have to go looking for it, unless they are very lucky. The pity is, though, that often religious education avoids the hard core of its subject — the *truths* of faith, food for the Christian mind which we can keep drawing on as we make our way through life. So if you happen to be still getting religion classes, try not to be messed around with. If your religion teacher asks you for your views on world population; on the rightful owners of the land; on civil strife in some distant country; on whether priests should wear civvies; or whether it is better

12 *About believing*

to stop going to Mass if you doubt the validity of the Faith: if he asks you this sort of thing do not give him an answer; ask him, as politely as you can, to teach you your religion; which is the one which he professes. Do not ask him for his views; ask him what the Church teaches; ask him to explain it, as best he can.

He will be only too happy to listen to you. He has been fumbling for the past few years, afraid that the teaching of the Church would be a 'hard saying' (cf. Jn 6:60), something you'd find difficult to take. And so each year he's given you less religion, less natural religion, less philosophy, less potted philosophy. Soon all that's left will be party politics. And all the time you all could have been 'becoming gods' (cf. Jn 10:34 and Ps 83:6)

REASONABLE FAITH

I am exaggerating. You can't be taught into holiness — but you can be taught out of it. If you have not taken in true ideas, true beliefs, you stand no chance of turning them into true living. If you have received a good doctrinal training then you have an even chance of a good life.

Religion really is about life — not about truths 'in the air'. In fact, to grasp your religion adequately you have to put it into practice. If you don't, then it's very likely that you'll sooner or later regard the whole thing as unreal. Apologetics, the rational 'argumentation' of the faith, has its importance (much under-estimated at present because people are more often than not trying to explain their own views, not the faith of the Church, and they have more limited intellectual capacity than that of the combined tradition of the Church); it can show the faith is reasonable, or not unreasonable. But it has only a secondary importance. We profess in the Creed that the Church is one, holy, catholic and apostolic; and the last great Council (Vatican II) taught that 'this Church [the Church founded by Jesus], constituted and organised as a society in the present world, subsists in the catholic Church, which is governed by the successor of Peter and by the bishops in communion with him';[2] we study what this Church teaches; but this does not mean that any one of us can carry around in his intellect, neatly organised, water-tight arguments in defence of the Faith. Our intelligence is too limited for that. Some of us are especially dense, others somewhat less so; that is all. But this, happily, does not mean that we are less whole Christians by reason of our mere intellectual shortcomings, or even memory defects. Do you think the early Christians entered into detailed arguments in their apostolate? St Paul does say: 'Be tactful with those who are not Christians and be sure that you make the best use of time with them. Talk to them agreeably and with a flavour of wit, and try to fit your answers to the needs of each one' (Col 4:5-6), but he boasts that 'in my speeches and sermons, there was none of the arguments that belong to philosophy' (1 Cor 2:4), and warns even the pastor Timothy to have 'nothing to do with pointless philosophical discussions' (2 Tim 2:16), and thanks 'God who, wherever he goes, makes us, in Christ, partners of his triumph, and through us is spreading the knowledge of himself, like a sweet smell, everywhere' (2 Cor 1:14-15). 'I did the planting, Apollo did the watering, but God made things grow' (1 Cor 3:6): God does the spreading.

Do not misunderstand me. I don't want to recommend to you any kind of anti-intellectual fundamentalism (in recent years many young Catholics, idealistic but under-educated in their faith, have been wandering up that kind of cul-de-sac, joining sects and 'cults', entering 'Hotel Californias' which have no exit doors); I simply want to remind you that being a good Catholic has not a great deal to do with having a neat, nicely argued answer to every question. Where we lack argument we should of course try to acquire it. But *answers* are more important than *arguments*.

It is more important to believe in the Eucharist, to hold that it is the body and the blood, the soul and the divinity of Christ, than to be able to explain how transubstantiation is metaphysically possible.

The early Christians did not run around with metaphysical arguments. They, rather, passed on the Good News that Christ was risen. They did not try to change the News to make it more palatable to pleasure-loving pagans; they lived, or tried to live, by the tradition they had received from the first disciples and which the Apostles and priests monitored. St Paul (a teacher specially chosen by God for the whole Church and a great intellectual) put it very plainly: 'While the Jews demand miracles and the Greeks look for wisdom [philosophy], here are we preaching a crucified Christ; to the Jews an obstacle that they cannot get over, to the pagans madness, but to those who have been called, whether they are Jews or Greeks, a Christ who is the power and the wisdom of God'(1 Cor 1:22-24).

Since that time God has made no new revelation; though we may know *better*, through the development of doctrine, we do not know *more* than the early Christians; there is no new gnosis, no further secret knowledge to be found which will render this particular message obsolete. Discourage people from spending their lives, or part of them, trying to change the Church; tell them that the Church is there to help them change themselves.

'Many today would argue that one is entitled, on grounds of conscience and in some fundamental matter, to choose a viewpoint contrary to that taught by the Church. Perhaps; but what one is not entitled to do, after such a choice, is to insist on regarding one's new position as a Catholic position. Such insistence is not to demand freedom; or if it is, it is to demand the freedom to empty terms and positions of any real meaning.

'To claim the right both to be called a Catholic and to be totally subjective about what being a Catholic means, is a particularly modern phenomenon — one that may not be due to insincerity, but that must be put down to a lack of thought, to a failure to understand that to be a Catholic means to belong — voluntarily — to a Body that, where fundamental principles are concerned, thinks and teaches with the mind of Christ'[3].

'There cannot be more than one Good News; it is merely that some trouble-makers among you want to change the Good News of Christ' (Gal 1:7-8).

IT IS EASY NOT TO BELIEVE

You have only to look around you and you will see how easy it is not to believe. If you do not want to believe in the teaching of the catholic Church, just try. It is certainly easy for non-Christians and even non-Catholic Christians not to believe in it; they have not been educated to do so. But it is easy also for Catholics. If you want not to believe, just start picking holes in anything or everything the Pope says; a little effort and you will soon only believe those things which you like to believe in, those things you, with your particular psychology and background, take to readily. If you are an ordinary sort of person you will not at first take issue with the doctrine of the Trinity but rather with some aspect of the moral teaching of the Church: depending on your inclinations or taste for exploration you will decide — as if it depended on your say-so! — that it is 'almost impossible' to commit a mortal sin; and armed with this licence you will try to regard as mere defects what are really whoppers. And even if you do not choose to go off the rails yourself, you will be quite easily convinced that people have a 'right' (!) to do so, and you will go out of your way to convenience them. Criticise, read criticism, encourage criticism and — especially in today's environment — soon you will be able not to believe.

Whereas St Paul says, arrogantly, 'the gospel will save you only if you keep believing exactly what I preached to you — believing anything else will not lead to anything' (1 Cor 15:2). He says that the only chance you have of believing is (1) to want to believe and (2) to stick to the tradition.

If you choose not to believe, you are not really rejecting 'mysteries'. For even on the human level 'what can be known about God is perfectly plain; ever since God created the world his everlasting power and deity — however invisible — have been there for the mind to see in the things that he has made. By closing your eyes you make nonsense out of logic and your mind is darkened. The more you call yourself a philosopher the stupider you become. God leaves you to your irrational ideas and to your monstrous behaviour. And so you are steeped in all kinds of depravity, rottenness, greed and malice and addicted to envy, murder, treachery and spite. Libellers, slanderers, enemies of God, rude, arrogant and boastful, enterprising in sin, rebellious to parents, without brains, honour, love or pity. You know what God's verdict is: that those who behave like this deserve to die — and yet they do it; and what is worse, encourage others to do the same' (in Rom 1:19-32).

What St Paul is saying here is this: if you close your eyes to the existence of a personal God and build up your very own philosophy, seeking yourself instead of truth, you will soon become a candidate for condemnation. And *then* you will be classically ripe to be on the receiving end of the exact kind of apostolate which the early Christians did. But what a waste that would imply: you, as a Christian, are already equipped by God to be an apostle yourself.

BUT THE WORLD CAN NEVER BE 'WON'

Another easy way to lose your faith is by *being demoralised*, which is like being beaten before you start. You can be demoralised by your own sins and failings (whether you take them too seriously and too secretly in adolescence, or too lightly as a 'mature' adult) or by the sins and failings of others. Nowadays, when the 'news' thrust at us on all sides tends to highlight violence and aberration, we can very easily feel like saying 'What's the use? Christianity is fighting a losing battle. It does not work.'

That argument has been doing the rounds since the Church began. Besides, the success of Christianity can never be gauged by statistics. Without any arrogance or naivety, the Christian who really tries is the taste-giving salt of the earth; he is the leaven which raises all the dough; his good life, a supernatural life, repairs and makes up for the faults of the natural lives of countless other people. Just as Christ, the first-born among many brethren, opened the way to salvation for all men, the Christians by their simple living faith and their solidarity with all men apply that salvation to their world.

Anyway, do not think too much about the world! the world! That is the great escape-route of our time, the way to shed all personal responsibility. Think rather of *your* world, the only world you will ever be involved in; a world which is restricted — as far as your *external* activity is concerned — to a relatively few people with whom you are in fairly close contact. God, who has made you a Christian, wants you to *be* a Christian right there, where you are. If you are faithful, he will make you fruitful.

BUT MY CONSCIENCE...

I would hate in any way to force your conscience, to pressurize you. But I feel no freedom to say: OK, go ahead, push aside your religious background, taste every dish, and when you're jaded, then (young or middle-aged or old) go looking for God; he will still be there, an eye out for the prodigal son. You appeal to conscience, to protect yourself against the Church, the priests, your parents, even your friends? Then to conscience you shall go. Try this line of advice: 'Cardinal Newman is frequently invoked today, and rightly so, as one of the main exponents of the "supremacy of conscience". His *Letter to the Duke of Norfolk* (1874) contains the famous phrase "If I am obliged to bring religion into after-dinner toasts (which indeed does not seem quite the thing) I shall drink — to the Pope, if you please. Still, to Conscience first, and to the Pope afterwards".

'But, in defending the supremacy of conscience, he is very explicit as to *what sort* of conscience can be regarded as supreme, and as to *what must be our attitude* towards its supremacy: conscience understood "not as a fancy or an opinion, but as a *dutiful obedience* to what claims to be a Divine voice speaking within us" (Newman again). Many of those who invoke Newman today, on this matter of the rights of conscience, fail to echo his emphasis on the *duties* of conscience, on the duties owed *towards* conscience. In his *Apologia* he writes, "I have always contended that obedience even to an erring conscience was the way to gain light". No doubt he felt he was speaking from personal experience. And anyone familiar with his life knows how he suffered from his immensely sensitive *obedience* to his conscience, how he suffered as it brought him to the light.

'Today, more than ever, it is necessary to say that the man who really listens to his conscience and is prepared to be faithful to it, will often have the sense of *obeying* a voice that leads him *in a direction a large part of him does not feel like following*. We are of course speaking of the man who takes his conscience seriously, who looks up to

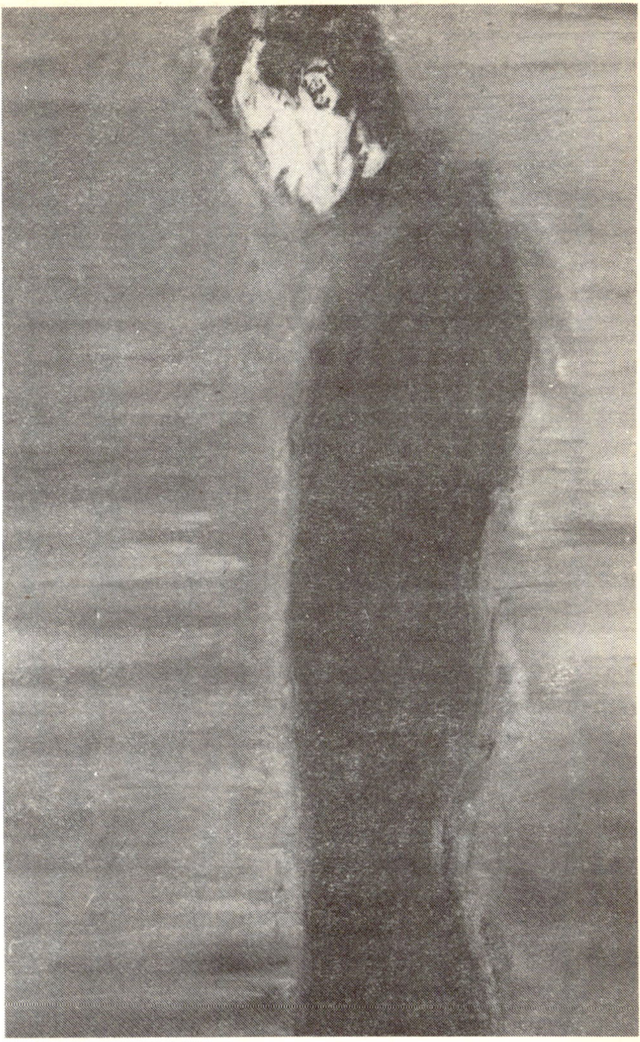

it and respects it; and for this reason is prepared to acknowledge its supremacy and obey it.

'Newman writes elsewhere that if we wish to find religious (or moral) truth, we need to "interrogate our hearts, and (since it is a personal individual matter) interrogate our *own* hearts — interrogate our own conscience, interrogate, I will say, the God who dwells there", and to do so "with an earnest desire to know the truth and a sincere intention of following it".

'Conscience is a precious but delicate guide. Its voice is easily distorted or obscured. To dictate to conscience is to silence and, eventually, to destroy it. Conscience must be listened to, and listened to sensitively. It needs to be interrogated, even to be cross-examined. And only those who habitually interrogate their conscience and are ready to pay heed even to its awkward answers, will not cheat their conscience or be cheated by it'.[4]

IT IS EASY TO BELIEVE

It is easy to believe: if you want to believe; if you are well-disposed; if your attitude is an active one. If *you* want to believe, to follow through on the baptism you have received, the formula is simple: (1) 'Repent' (Mk 1:15), (2) seek to know what the Church, not some theologian or journalist (however competent) teaches; (3) build up your Christian life by prayer and the sacraments, getting to know Jesus Christ; (4) and then follow St Paul's advice and 'offer your living bodies as a holy sacrifice ...; let your behaviour change, modelled by your new mind, not on the behaviour of the world around you.... Sincerely prefer good to evil.... Love each other as much as brothers should.... Work for the Lord with untiring effort.... Treat everyone with equal kindness.... Resist evil and conquer it with good.... Obey the civil authorities.... Be brave and strong.... We are God's work of art, created in Christ

Jesus to live the good life as from the beginning he had meant us to live it.... Make a point of living quietly, attending to your own business and earning your living' (Rom 12:1ff; 1 Cor 16:13; Eph 2:10; 1 Thess 4:11). Hardly a limited panorama. The world is the oyster of this Christian and it is easy to see how quickly its values would be turned upside down if more people's lives were based on these truths. The radicalism which thus effortlessly results from Christianity leaves human radical formulae sounding like a child's whinge. To put it more accurately, it is easy to know how to *go about* believing. You have God's help: it deserves the response of your best effort. Even the pain (which must come in one way or another), the difficulty (which could take the form of doubt, at times), is swallowed up in the joy of serving God. But don't think of this business as a nice, cosy mystical relationship between yourself and a God 'out-there' or even an indwelling God:

SHOULD CHRISTIANS GIVE GOOD EXAMPLE?

There is a tendency for people to think that the function of bishops, priests and other officials is to preach; and the function of lay people to be (1) preached at and (2) to 'behave'. To put it another way, the Christian in the street has a serious duty to give good example (understood in an almost spectral sense). Forget it! You have a mouth, a tongue. Just 'being there' — coy, demure, edifying behaviour — is not enough (in fact it is even humanly unbecoming). We must be confessors and professors of the faith; but in our own way. 'On all Christians rests the noble obligation of working to bring all men throughout the whole world to hear and accept the divine message of salvation' (as Vatican II puts it).[5] You do it particularly through your friendship and your natural relationships: you don't have to set yourself up as a teacher of your peers.

22 *About believing*

Look: the Church tells us that even 'children [much younger than you] have an apostolate of their own. In their own way they are true living witnesses of Christ among their companions'.[6] Do not dare open your mouth if you are not *trying* to be a good Christian. And if you are trying, do not dare *not* to open that mouth of yours.

The same old story

Suppose I'm giving a Christian doctrine lesson.

If I propose that two and two are four, most of you will agree. If I say 'God is a father' you will ask me to explain myself before you can think of agreeing. Your intelligence and will and emotions all come into your reaction. You are all different, all unique, each with his or her qualities, kinks, hang-ups, prejudices, background, knowledge, intelligence. And each of you has his own grace, his own state of relationship with God, with Christ.

Yet though you are all different you are also all the same; you are 'normal' or ordinary people. You have ordinary human reactions to things and people. And you share group attitudes. These are attitudes common to your group; some of them derive from that group; some have even been *imposed* by the group and accepted by you due to laziness or lack of personality. You don't want to be different, you want to hide in the crowd, so you conform to patterns which other people set; you are a follower of fashion — maybe the fashion of not being fashionable. It is one thing to conform — even if you have to make an effort — when valid authority lays down the law (for example, trying to keep within the speed limit) but it is ridiculous to conform to the attitudes of a crowd or to obey the dictates of a manipulator. So many 'hard' men are really very soft.

I HAVE A JOB TO DO
Well, I have to *teach* you religion and as long as you are ready to stay in my class you have to *learn* it. That's the set-up. Teaching religion, imparting religious knowledge, is not just a matter of communicating facts. But it is partly

that. If you want to become a mathematician you must study mathematics; to be good at French you must work at it; and to have religious knowledge you must learn about God. Indeed, this need to learn is particularly true in the case of the Church: as far as Christian doctrine is concerned it has to be *handed on*. Genuine Christian doctrine has been handed on from one generation to another. You cannot have it unless you take it and make it your own. You can't get it unless it's given to you. If you are not to waste your time in these classes you must ask me not what I think about this or that question but rather what — if anything — does the Church teach about it.

One tendency in particular I'd warn you against: that of thinking that in order to acquire religious knowledge you must test everything the Church says against your spontaneous reactions as if the touchstone of truth were your own instant, 'authentic' response to what you hear. What is so sure, so correct, about the bizarre collection of opinions, prejudices, hunches, facts, experiences which go to make up your instinctive reactions — or mine? Yet this is the 'method' which lies at the basis of a widespread method of religious education known as 'values clarification'. You may not be familiar with the *name* of this method but there is quite a good chance that the method has been used on you. In essence, as far as objective values or truths are concerned, it is the very reverse of a method *of education* because it is designed by its inventors to 'liberate' the individual from any notion of objective truth; the only values they know are emotions, and sheer emotions do not build a real man, a real woman, and cannot make a Christian.

I could pander to your spontaneous reactions, I could try to be a manipulator, and give you instant Christianity. But if I played the hot gospeller in that way I would turn the class into a kind of sermon; a few might be impressed,

I have a job to do 25

won over, 'converted' (with every chance that when they go out into the sun the effects would evaporate). If on the other hand I played the intellectual, the reasoner, we would get caught in a permanent circuit of philosophies and arguments and ifs and buts (you would get no Christian knowledge — only some 'Christian information', data for small talk); I would be short-changing you.

I'm going to try to steer a middle course. It aims at explaining the teachings of the Church and showing you, who are Christians, Catholics, a Christian panorama of life and of the world. I'm going to assume a germ of belief. If your faith is weak, well, let's see if we honestly can't make it stronger; if it is strong, let's try to understand it better. You who are not a Catholic: do stay if you wish.

You who are smart must realise that you can never understand your religion if you want continually to try to pick holes in it: a person who is clever in that sort of way is proud and arrogant. If you are proud towards Christianity you'll never understand it. If you are proud towards God he won't play either: he has 'routed the proud of heart' (Lk 1:51). Try not to be proud: you will never be yourself that way, never mind a good Christian. (Try approaching chemistry in that negative frame of mind: you won't even get a basic pass.)

And you who are simple and uncomplicated: be clever in that other sense. You have a duty to think. St Paul tells you, 'You are not to be childish in your outlook. You can be babies as far as wickedness is concerned, but mentally you must be adult' (1 Cor 14:21-22). You have a duty to think: stretch your mind. We have to express our love of God not just in goodish behaviour: we have to love him also *with our whole mind*; we have to express that love not just by prayer but also by the way we put our time to good use and the way we treat the people we meet. A lot of people we have contact with won't have a strong hold on

26 *The same old story*

the faith. St Peter reminds us always to 'have your answers ready for people who ask you the reason for the hope you all have' (1 Pet 3:15). We need to be able to give some kind of explanation for the faith we hold. It is a reasonable thing, though it outstrips reason or human science. We can never know God enough, or the ways to him.

A MODERN CHRISTIANITY?

You must not expect from me way-out ideas, any kind of message which even *seems* to be at odds with what you might take from a reading of the Gospel or the New Testament. No fashionable Christianity. No whole new insight. The only news I have is the Good News: that is all about Christ, a man who was God, the Alpha and Omega, the beginning of all things and their end. He is the peak of God's self-revelation to men. In religion there is no progress in the sense that you might say there is progress in technology: it's all happened.[7] But this 'old news' is never stale, for Christ, even the man Christ, is not a historical figure. He is risen! He is alive! He *is* today as yesterday or in two thousand years time. He is both rooted in history and above history, above time and space, unlimited.

Do you find that difficult to believe? Well, that's the *starting point* as far as a Christian is concerned. What first identifies the Christian is his stand on the faith. 'I believe in one God, the Father almighty ... and in Jesus Christ.... On the third day he rose from the dead as the scriptures had foretold ... And in the Holy Spirit ... and in the Church ...'. All these Christians (not only Catholics) own up to this. That — imagine! — is the *starting point*.

And it is worth pointing out that a Christian's baptism equips him to make this act of faith. It has endowed him with the supernatural gift of faith, a form of *certain* knowledge, knowledge based on the authority of God who has revealed this knowledge to him, and happily not based on the always imperfect reasoning of a human being. In Peter Shaffer's play, *The Royal Hunt of the Sun*, this faith is expressed very vividly by Pizarro's young equerry when he tries to dissuade his master from believing that the Inca can, if he takes his own life, be resurrected by the next morning's sun. The equerry argues that only Christ could and did raise himself from the dead. 'Do you really *believe* that?', Pizarro asks him. 'Yes, my lord, I believe on my soul. I believe with perfect faith.' That is the kind of faith that is available to Christians; that is the true basis of Christian living.

Have you heard that Christianity, the Church, is changing? Forget it. Don't think that some time, later on, the Church is going to catch up with you. You are — I am — way behind. We have to follow Christ and he, who is unchanging, is ahead of us. He has gone on ahead; don't wait for him to come round again with some new doctrine; some more congenial story; some less outrageous, some less incredible story.

RELIGIOUS PRACTICE

I'm sorry, but if you want to be a Christian *you have to pray* and you have to try to pray always. You have to turn to God with your hands empty, realising that you need him. Do you plan to wait until your stomach is empty, or you've lost your job, or you're paralysed, or dying, or all washed up, or you're retired and have time for him? Don't kid yourself: you won't realise you need him then either.

I'm sorry, but you have to go to Mass on Sunday (or Saturday night). I don't care how much 'good work' you do; how socially involved you are; how short you are on sleep; how rather inconvenient it is: you have to go to Sunday Mass if you are to practise as a Catholic; even if you are not in the 'state of grace'. You commit a mortal sin by just passing up Sunday Mass. It's just one aspect of your Christian practice but it's an important one. The Church effectively says: if you don't do this minimum practice you are cutting yourself off from the community; you are in line for deterioration; this minimum is so important that I'm labelling it a mortal sin to stay away. This practice goes right back to the early Church. (Similarly you must go to Communion at least once a year, around Easter. Another tall order? Another intolerable intrusion on your time and lifestyle?)

CENSORSHIP

I'm sorry, but you may not read (or watch on TV or video or at the cinema) everything you feel like. To take one example, you may not read heretical books. If you were a heretic then *maybe* you could also pick and choose to suit your taste (that's what 'heresy' means); but if you want to be an orthodox Catholic, upright, coherent, faithful, who can say the Creed standing up, then you must be careful about what you take into your soul and mind. If you are in doubt consult someone more learned than yourself who has the same ideals as your own. The Church for some four hundred years had an 'Index' of prohibited books which no Catholic might read without permission. Notice how intellectual the Church is: it is concerned about the influence of ideas (people who dismiss such norms really imply that you can't be influenced in that way; certainly my own experience disproves that, as should the whole idea of education). So, as far as religion is concerned, read only 'good books'. (If you are studying comparative religion or dealing with unorthodox material you have to be especially alert that heresy does not seep in.) That 'Index' grew unwieldly and out of date so the Church took away the penalty it implied (it's still there, as a rather outdated reference); but at the same time it stresses that you have a personal obligation not to read harmful material. Do you want to read whatever you like? Do so: it is exactly the same thing as *doing* whatever you like. Do you want to do whatever you like? Forget about being a Christian.

Do you want to read corrupt books. To find out, to get a second-hand thrill? The author of the sentimental novel *Love Story* put it quite nicely when asked why he didn't lard his fiction with sex: 'As I see it two people make love, four people (the two plus the author and the reader) make an orgy.'

GOOD USE OF YOUR TIME

I'm sorry, but if you want to be a Christian you must never be idle. There is no such thing as a holiday from Christianity, a holiday from God, time out all for yourself. You must deny yourself, say 'no' to yourself. Take up your cross and follow him. Everything you do must be relatable to God — your sleep, your rest, your leisure, your work, your loves, your drink, your food, your social life: all these human values, these good things, must be flavoured with self-denial. It is — haven't you heard — the salt of perfection.

I'm sorry, but even if you can't get a job when you leave school (criminal, isn't it, that man who was made to work should be deprived of the opportunity: what could be more *natural* than for everyone to have an opportunity to shape the world): even if you can't get a job and have to sign on for unemployment benefit: even then you have no right to hang around, cultivating idleness.

YOUR BODY

I'm sorry, but you must wait until you are married. That is the only context in which a Christian can have sex. And he has to check the genuineness, the validity, of his spontaneity against a law which is outside him — the natural law — which the Church interprets in an unchanging way. The early Christians lived in a decadent environment and survived as Christians, and we have to do the same. Masturbation, homosexual activity, sex outside marriage, contraception, abortion and the lot: these are not new, natural responses of people to the 'pressures of the modern age'. They are *old* sins, always old, always sins. Do not be surprised, then, if you are tempted to them: but do reject them. 'You know perfectly well,' St Paul told the Christians in swinging Corinth, 'that people who do wrong will not inherit the kingdom of God: people of immoral lives, idolators, adulterers, catamites, sodomites, thieves, usurers, drunkards, slanderers and swindlers will never inherit the kingdom of God. These are the sort of people some of you were once, but now you have been washed clean, and sanctified, and justified through the name of the Lord Jesus Christ...' (1 Cor 6:9-11). 'The body — this is not meant for fornication; it is for the Lord, and the Lord for the body.... You know, surely, that your bodies are members making up the body of Christ; do you think I can take parts of Christ's body and join them to the body of a prostitute? Never! ... Keep away from fornication. All the other sins are committed outside the body; but to fornicate is to sin against your own body. Your body, you know, is a temple of the Holy Spirit, who is in you since you received him from God. You are not your own property; you have been brought and paid for. That is why you should use your body for the glory of God' (1 Cor 6:13-20). What a marvellous invitation to marriage: to use your body for the glory of God! At the present time society *is* paying a high price in the form of the scourge of AIDS. I don't know what the origin of AIDS is, but we all know that sexual promiscuity is a main channel of spreading it. Even so, people are being told blandly, 'If you insist on having sex, do be careful' and in some places they are actually being handed out free contraceptives — a public invitation to sin; the result is that, paradoxically, the presence of death in sex is leading to actual promotion (by governments, hotels, 'liberationist' lobbies) of casual sex.

The 'natural law' does not apply just to Catholics. The need for it is part and parcel of man's true nature; if people ignore it or are ignorant of it they will get into a mess and society sooner or later will pay for it.

People may, and do, choose to ignore the natural law but they have no fundamental, inalienable right to do so, no right which the State's law (about which God too is concerned) has a duty to foster. Society cannot — as history will show you — legislate people into goodness, but it can, if it chooses, try to deter people from evil. Thus the fact that some countries legalise abortion or the sale of contraceptives or try to keep the population down is simply a political phenomenon. If society goes along with them, it has done a bad thing. Don't think that as a Christian you have any duty to facilitate sinful behaviour in that way. Don't thing that as a free man you have a duty to promote 'freedom' of that sort. On the contrary. (Neither, of course, do you have a right to take the law into your own hands and throw bombs at 'bad people', but you will have a duty as a voter or perhaps even as a politician to affect the shape of the law.)

POVERTY

Did you notice what St Paul said there: 'You are not your own property'? If I don't own myself, how much less a right do I have to own things.... This is all the ammunition you need to give the lie to those superficial accusations that 'the Church' is allied to 'capitalism', or to the argument that the Church should embrace communism. A Christian, no matter what system, what social structure, he happens to be living and working in, is — or should be — the enemy of all ideologies. He must have no such idols for, by living the consequences of his faith, he and his brothers and sisters can turn the system inside out.

So, I'm sorry, you have to be poor; no matter how rich you are, you must be poor. No, it's not the Sultan of Brunei or the Rockefellers or the housewife with the second Mercedes who have to be poor. It is you, you who have a weekly allowance from your parents, or the remains of your summer earnings. It is you who, in *your* plenty, have to be poor. Even when you have the sports car you have to be poor; otherwise your cannot be a Christian, a saint. You must venerate all the little or big things you have; you must *enjoy the responsibility* of ownership; you must not cry like a spoilt child if the State — later on — taxes your luxuries, controls your profit distribution, limits your land rights in a clumsy attempt to spread the wealth of the world more evenly.

Two things, then, on poverty: (1) *you* must strive to be poor no matter how well off you may appear to be;(2) you have a responsibility towards other people to try to see that they have access to the world's wealth. The first is manifestly within your reach. The second is more difficult of achievement, but whatever your position in society you must do what you can to achieve it.

Don't make the mistake of thinking there are only three kinds of poverty — that of the religious who surrender ownership and live a community life; and that of easy-come, easy-go dreaming people; and that of people 'below the poverty line'. *All* Christians have to be poor; and the highway to poverty can carry most of us a long way. The trouble is we don't realise we're on it. For example:

Student: if you want to be poor, the real 'poor student': put in a good day's work.

Worker: pay has to be earned; you have to give of your best. The worker whose eye is only on the pay-packet — he's the one who is 'rich'.

Parent: don't calculate so meanly; have another child, it's a great way to be poor.

Invalid: you can be poor by being good enough to let people help you.

Wife: you can learn from those great ladies in the Old Testament who seemed to have no time for themselves: all their energies in some way or other went to enhance their family. And as time goes on you may have to work a little more on yourself, on the 'facade', to be attractive (your body is your husband's): that, oddly enough, is a way to be poor. Who said poverty was ... slovenly?

Husband: you have your family to think of. Spend reasonably what you can on your children's growth and education. You don't have to accumulate, hoarding for a rainy day; there's no law that says you have to endow them with every latest plaything (they'll much prefer your company, your friendship), much less leave them fat legacies. And *your* body is your wife's; so don't abuse it.

Owner: take care. You are a caretaker. The Church tells you have a right to private property — you need some living room; a space for yourself and your family; a place to call your own. Yet even if it is a castle, you're not really lord of all you survey. Property is a responsibility, a liability. You have to answer for it. Even if it is a modest little place you still have to answer for it; and that you do by keeping it clean and tidy and attractive; by making things last; by fixing the plug; and putting out the garbage. And maybe you could have a rather open house, where your friends and your children's friends will always find a welcome.

Hospitality is a form of poverty — it shows that you own things *for* other people.

The highway to poverty: giving yourself, spending yourself; and restricting the use you make of things (interesting, how 'environmentalist' Christian poverty is).

In his letter on the 'Development of Peoples', addressed to 'the bishops, priests, religious, the faithful and to all men of good will', Pope Paul VI in connection with property quoted St Ambrose (who wrote *before the Dark Ages*, c.380 AD): 'You are not handing over to him what is his. For what has been given in common for the use of all, you have arrogated to yourself. The world is given to all, and not only to the rich'. That is, private property does not constitute for anyone an absolute and unconditioned right. No one is justified in keeping for his exclusive use what he does not need, when others lack necessities.... If there should arise a conflict 'between acquired private rights and primary community exigencies', it is the responsibility of public authorities, the Pope pointed out, 'to look for solutions, with the active participation of individuals and social groups'.[8]

But I beg you: do not relax in your personal comfort and throw stones at society and State. How much 'revolution' is the work of envious and greedy men who become the new establishment once they get power....

DRINK

I'm sorry, but you must not get drunk; you must not joke that 'he was stoned out of his mind'. That is a sinful disregard for your own self-control, for that body which is the Lord's, for the guy who made the beer for your enjoyment.

SIN

I'm sorry, therefore, but there *is* such a thing as sin. People can and do, constantly, get better or worse. People can offend (sin) not just against society or their family or friends or their own bodies or minds: in so doing they offend God, they put obstacles between themselves and him as clearly as too much alcohol separates them from their better selves. And they — you and I — are responsible for these offences; they are not caused by some traumatic experience in adolescence or early infancy or by the misdemeanours of your grandfather before you were born or by a society which has frustrated the development of your talent. *We sin*; and we can do so in such a serious way that we really do cut ourselves off from friendship with God: we become estranged. He becomes 'foreign' to us, and sometimes we do not even bother to try to work out why.

FORGIVENESS

I'm sorry, but in these circumstances it is *not* good enough for you as a Catholic to take a deep breath, put on a hangdog look, thump your breast — privately, or at Mass, or in some group session — and tell God you're sorry. For he has set up a system which objectivises the whole business of forgiveness. It is called the sacrament of penance or reconciliation. And it is there to be availed of, by obligation (yes, rules!), when you have sinned seriously; and, *not* by obligation, as a source of particular grace, in a regular way, since you need help to overcome your inclination to evil. You can't dismiss evil as a medieval superstition. It is something provoked constantly by yourself, by your surroundings and by the Devil. (The Devil is not just a myth, to be used to make horror films; he is a real live person.) Evil is something to be acknowledged as committed not just by society and politicians but by you. And it's something to be shed by seeking and receiving forgiveness.

ADMIT IT

Don't try to pretend that the forbidden things that you, you in particular, are attracted to are really not all that bad. Admit that they are bad. Even if you do them because, like everything, they contain some good, some partial fragile good, even then as a first Christian step admit that you could have done wrong. 'I have sinned' is the beginning of holiness, one could almost say. For, once a person recognises his defectivity he is knocking on the door of forgiveness. And if he recognises that he cannot heal himself and then turns to the Christian's God naked and ashamed, the fatted calf will be killed and he will be feasted by his Father. Christ has set the whole thing up. It is, as I have just said, the sacrament of pardon: there you put on Jesus Christ. Do you want to know a good apostolate for an ordinary Christian? (1) Let him have many friends and bad ones and (2) let him lead them, cajole them, 'drag' them to confession. So much hot air, puerile bravado, problems of faith, problems of love, problems of the mind, are healed by that sacrament. You will also — and this too is a value but it's another story — by going to confession (*often*) liberate so many good priests from the frustration of 'social work', 'youth work', 'liturgical experimentation', 'seminars', 'psychology', 'sociology', if you approach them as you would Christ and seek forgiveness. In the sacrament of reconciliation you find through the priest's mind and words the healing touch of Christ.

EUCHARIST

And then you can receive the body and blood of the Lord, the power of God: the Creator, the Spirit, who would live in you as in a temple. Not just a philosophy which stretches your mind, not some oriental 'way' to control yourself or lose yourself, not an ideology which warps your life, not a nice idea which burns out next week, not a drug trip, not a ditty which lasts 3.6 minutes, but Christ, the beginning of all things and their end. 'In the days to come [now, after the Resurrection] I will pour out my spirit on all mankind. Their sons and daughters shall prophesy, your young men shall see visions, your old men shall dream dreams' (Acts 2:17).[9]

LOOK AROUND

I'm not saying this to have you turn into hot little souls living a special, private, holy world of your own. You must live in *this* world; with your own personality and character, your own qualities and defects. No: this Christian vision which infects your reaction to everything is in itself a responsibility: you do not own it, you must give it away. You must own up to it, communicating it to your friends and colleagues. If it destroys you then it's not authentic. If all these 'bad' friends reject you then you haven't understood anything. A Christian is not a freak. He is a man. In fact he is the epitome of man, the norm. Men created by God and sinners against him and redeemed by Christ and endowed with grace *are* men. Men created by God and sinners against him and seekers after themselves are subjects for gentle pity. You (Christ) must free them from that pitiful condition. You (Christ) must cure their blindness and lameness and leprosy and dumbness. Who do you think are going to do it? Angels? They are your helpers. Priests? They are just other Christians, equal Christians, with a very specialised job to do, which they can't do without the cooperation of the Christian community. Bishops? Popes? You — or we — the very last, the very least in the kingdom of God: you are Christ who is risen.

HAVING GOTTEN THAT OFF MY CHEST

So don't make me keep my cool; don't let me be just a

teacher of a subject. Don't expect me to be a teacher of philosophy or theology. Let me try to be a Christian. And then let's use our wits to understand our faith.

And to begin with, let's see if we can work out the existence of God. A lot of people seem to be having trouble on that score. . . .

The four horsemen of the Apocalypse: war, pain, hunger, violence

Sometime around 1600 the Bishop-in-exile of Geneva (for Catholics had been ousted by Calvinists), operating from across the border in France, wrote a book called *Introduction to the Devout Life*. I know, the title is off-putting; but if you ignore it and the antique style of the book, you, even you, will find it interesting and helpful.

Anyway, when St Francis de Sales wrote it it immediately became a bestseller among the reading public. It took its place alongside and maybe even replaced what had been the staple diet of devout Christians for over one hundred years, *The Imitation of Christ* (a book with a noticeable monastic background). The secret of its success was that it taught that even ladies who powdered their noses and wore satin and had husbands, and gentlemen who engaged in affairs of court, state or business, could be not *mere* Christians but really first-class Christians, saints.

Read Francis de Sales' book quietly, intelligently and humbly: it can do you good. I know better books, but that one has a permanent place in Christian culture.

However, that's not what I wanted to talk about. You see, I was going to call this chapter 'An Introduction to the Hard Life', borrowing *that* title from a manuscript I heard of. It was also about making saints, not of courtiers but of young men whose staple diet is — according to the conventional image — sex, alcohol and violence. I never read the manuscript, so that's the end of my plagiarising. I wanted to write under that title but it took me so long to work around to the point that it will have to be the *next* chapter. This is a sort of *Introduction to an Introduction to the Hard Life*.

MY BEST WISHES

You have heard it said by Christ that the second greatest commandment is 'You must love your neighbour as yourself'. Well, we normally do like ourselves and treat ourselves well. *Therefore* for you and for myself I want the best. I want you to have enjoyment, revelry, happiness, joy, elation, thrill, fulfilment; there is nothing which will enhance you that I do not want you to have, whether it is a 'high' thing (all very spiritual) or a 'low' thing (back to nature: sun, sensation). And anything that would diminish you I'll try to keep at bay or distract you from.

For you, then, I wish death, for 'anyone who loses his life for my sake will find it' (Mt 11:39). For you I wish poverty because 'it will be hard for a rich man to enter the kingdom of heaven' (Mt 19:23). 'I will tell you which are man's treasures on earth so that you will not let them go to waste: hunger, thirst, heat, cold, pain, dishonour, poverty, loneliness, betrayal, slander, prison. . .'.[10] It sounds more like a curse than a blessing. No wonder Christianity is a bad business. St Teresa of Avila in one of her many rough passages (around 1570), when her carriage got swamped by a flood, gave out to Christ, saying, 'No wonder you have so few friends if this is the way you treat them!' I only recently realised that, if tradition is correct, of all those Apostles at the last supper all but two (John and Judas) died the violent death of a martyr. Jesus does not go out of his way to be popular, meek though he may be.

Listen to a man I knew who was always preaching a 'war of peace': 'I want you to be happy on earth. And you will not be happy if you don't lose that fear of suffering. For, as long as we are "wayfarers" it is precisely in suffering that our happiness lies'.[11]

Are these Christians masochists, and Christ the ringleader? Or are they simply Chestertonians all, playing with words, buying and selling paradoxes; ready to resort to anything to catch the attention of the passer-by?

WAR ON WANT

First let's clear the air. All these disagreeable things like war, death, pain, hunger etc. are bad. They are evil, deprivations, absence of due good. You should do what you can to eliminate them: your ideal, the Christian ideal, is one of service, putting people, other people, before yourself.

It is not enough to protest about what other people are doing. For example, it is all very well to confront war or armaments as a pacifist and walk around asking for peace; but at the same time you must at least be trying to get on with your parents whom you see as hidebound conservatives just because they are less worried by the world scene (and who may in fact be rather bourgeois, rather self-indulgent). It is alright to picket some embassy, but if hate can be read in your teeth it is yourself you are destroying, not some 'communist' or 'fascist' government which is trampling some minority. It is good to campaign for women's rights but at the same time you should not forget the rights of unborn babies — who are much less articulate and more in need of your help because many die before they are born.

Perhaps it's not very practicable to fight on all fronts; you have to specialise; your time is limited. Fine, then your cause should at least be a totally positive one: it would be crazy to join a platform for a women's rights group if that group advocated abortion. And it's always useful to look 'through' an association to make sure it's not a front: because if it's in any way unauthentic it surely can't be for you.

But even all these good things you're looking for — peace, plenty, ease — are not absolutes. It is good to avoid inflicting pain, but if you are a trainer you have to be demanding; people have gone to you precisely to be demanded of: they, in their sober moments, actually want you to put the pressure on because that's the only way to get nearer their goal. Similarly it is good to have peace, but: peace at any price? And even if no one were gunning for you or suppressing you, *mere* peace is arguably a bad thing; delivered from danger and installed in security people may go soft and languid, becoming (at best?) Oblomovs, dormice or (at worst?) creatively decadent.

Yet these distinctions are just refinements: any effort you or I or our community makes to rid people of deprivation is to be praised. For, it is all very well for me more or less freely to *choose* not to eat a lot of caviare, but it is quite different if I can't even get within reach of mere food, never mind eat enough.

But if you devote yourself exclusively to the liberation of the world from hunger, I must wonder whether you don't see a man as a mere stomach. Are you going to dedicate yourself entirely to filling stomachs? You will never succeed, for human problems are not solved by expenditure of energy. No matter how hard you work, if you put your faith in your own initiative, competence and energy *you will fail*. You need at least to attach yourself to some party or some ideology which is bigger than the individual: and some kind of 'philosophical' objective must provoke your enthusiasm and that of others. Perhaps (wait for it) some kind of force is called for. You may need to use violence to spread the national product more evenly: one horseman let loose to keep the others at bay. How did the Soviet Union solve its quartermastering problems in thirties: read *The Gulag Archipelago* (not a piece of churchy propaganda, but a catalogue of Soviet errors by a Nobel prizewinner) and you will find it liquidated millions of people.

And even if you and your colleagues did not fail, even if you eliminated all these deprivations, by cajoling and encouraging rather than liquidating, forcing and brainwashing: then what? You would have gotten rid of some painful physical inequalities; can you then take your ease, forsaking these 3,000,000,000 peaceful, fed, clothed, healthy people? Their freedom *from* those evils has only sense if they exercise their freedom *to* work and learn and love and pray: if they don't choose to act like that, then in another twenty years you'll have to turn out again, for there will be a whole new generation of greed, envy, sloth, gluttony, lust and pride re-creating pain and hunger and violence.

It's all rather demoralising, isn't it? Yet it is still good to try to make life more agreeable for other people. It is good to feed and clothe them, to give someone the better seat, the higher place, the affectionate glance, the warm smile. It is a Christian thing to strive to bring justice into the world and with it some minimum of security and wellbeing. A Christian, precisely because he has heaven as his goal, can put more energy and ingenuity into his effort 'to build the earthly city' than any non-believer can. How does the Christian achieve holiness? By sanctifying his work: by shaping the world which he has to 'dress and keep'. A Christian does not attain heaven by dreaming about heaven, by escaping from a disagreeable world, but by loving the earth and conversing with its Creator.[12]

You see, God got there before we did. He is not at all indifferent to the shaping of the world. He told us to 'dress and keep' the world. That's our 'thing'. Work is not a curse (though it's a taller order than he originally planned): neither should it become a disease, as if it had no purpose outside itself.

Work is — and only Christians can really make work all it ought to be —

a way to share in Creation;

a means of earning your living, developing your personality and expressing your talents and ideals;

a chance to serve your family, other people and society at large;

an opportunity of achieving solidarity with others and of putting down roots;

an environment for apostolate, a layman's apostolate with his peers and friends;

a way to become a saint, a proper place to find God, a good way to worship God (who is even ready to come to us if Christ offers him the 'fruit of the earth and work of human hands').

The best general, active method of solving 'the problems of the world' is: sanctify your work.

Don't be paralysed by the scale of the operation — the sameness of one day and the next and the next, the practically infinite difference between your effort and the scope that exists for it: it could cause you to switch off and opt out of any responsibility. What good could I do? What use am I? But: 'Have you seen how that imposing building was built? One brick after another. Thousands. But, one by one. And bags of cement, one by one. And blocks of stone, each of them insignificant compared with the massive whole. And beams of steel. And men working, the same hours, day after day. . . .

'Have you seen how that imposing buliding was built? . . . By dint of little things'.[13]

You have heard it said that the Church preaches 'Accept

your lot' and discourages people from improving the world: you heard wrong.

VICTIMISATION?
Yet, despite everyone's best efforts, you and I are involved in some *inescapable pain*. Let's take a quick look, each of us, not at the world for a moment: forget the killing fields, the torture and the prisons, the famines, the Arabs and the Jews; let's each look at himself or herself. Instead of being too tough to bother, take a good look at yourself in the mirror. Well, I'm terribly sorry; there's very little you can do about it. That face, you're stuck with it (barring accidents); those teeth, they may be still yours — or maybe not. That brain, not so brilliant. Those genes: you can't mutate them. Those instant reflexes of your mind and body: not all that controllable?

And then look around. Your parents; they can't be swopped. Your brothers and sisters: if you haven't got any, that's your hard luck; if you have, you'd better accept them.

Your choices, your opinions. Every choice is an entry into limitation. Next year you'll decide to study . . . law. Fine: you have just decided not to study medicine, anthropology, engineering; you are passing up farming, the army, travelling round the world on an oil tanker, making a living out of the guitar. . . . Sport: you're going to concentrate on middle-distance running. That's the end of the bicycle, the horse, the discus, rugby. Every free choice, every decision to overcome, to do better, to concentrate, every *commitment*, means a channelling of freedom. If you are to do those things well, then you are *not* to do a whole host of other things, good things, desirable things. For you have no time to be good at them, no time to give them, so limited are you.

See it as a kind of journey; you keep coming to forks

on the road. Of course, you can decide not to go on, to be paralysed by the problem of making a choice; angry at the injustice of having to make a choice. You can sit down and die away (not really a choice). No: the game is played by a kind of gambling. You choose to go to the left, so presumably you've lost out on all the possibilities which lay to the right.

When you think about it, it can be very frustrating. Why can't I be ten different things? Why can't I be a good lawyer and a good poet and a good architect? Why is the world *not* my oyster? Why do I have to choose? You are right. You want to be, to do, to taste everything, all at the same time; to have your options always open: it's quite natural, everyone has this capacity for infinity. We are a kind of god. In the beginning: 'God created man in his own image, in the image of God he created him'. Anything we lay hold of, unless it be God, is less than we're made for.

If you try to dodge this 'pain of limitation'; if you are angry against the fact that you are stupid or ugly or sensual; if you try to put your father out of your mind: you are making a bitter pill for yourself.

You have heard it said the Church preaches a message of acceptance: 'Accept your lot, the will of God.' It's true. And it's a true preaching. Unless you accept your real, objective limitations, including those really imposed by your own choices, unless you accept these data.... Don't just accept them, embrace them, boast about them; tell your Lord, 'Thank you for making me more stupid than most people'. Say 'yes' to your real limitations and the 'pain' of limitation turns instantly into a holy joy. You have heard no doubt Christ telling you that anyone who does not take his cross and follow in his footsteps is not worthy of him. Well, the first cross is this inescapable pain.

Dour Christians, frustrated Christians, mean Christians, small-minded Christians, sad Christians: Christians?

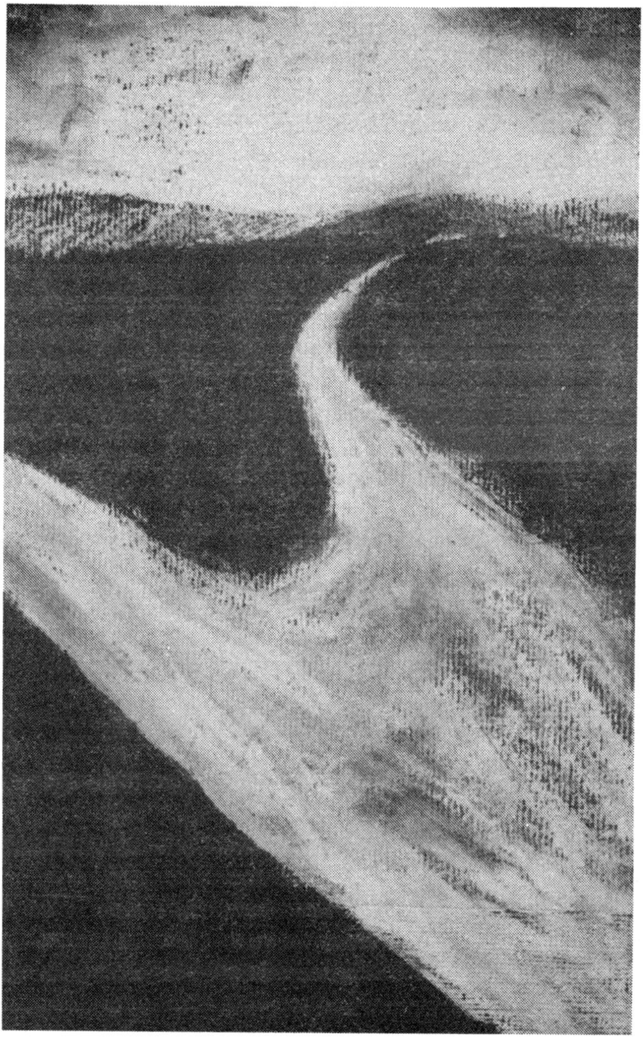

You are deprived, you are victimised? For a Christian there is only one victim. He is Christ, God who became a man to reconcile man to God by offering himself through his humanity. The Son of God, one in substance with the Father, is unlimited; yet *he* took on the limitation of humanity. He takes on all our limitations, becoming a kind of scapegoat. In his humanity he died and rose from the dead (that's what it's all about). He has enabled us to share God's life by grace. The time for moping is over, for God loves us, accepts us, as we are; it would then be unchivalrous to complain that we're mismade, some kind of mistake.

Everyone can say, now, sincerely, 'Here I am, Lord, for you have called me'. It is a beginning of wisdom.

PASSIVITY

A nice solution, isn't it, this one of acceptance — a joy which is the result of a change of attitude. Sorry: that is only the first chapter, the door, the beginning: an introduction to an introduction.

We are right to fight the four horsemen of the apocalypse. And we are wrong to fight God, who holds the ring. What about those good wishes I offered you: poverty, tears, hatred, injustice, dishonour?[14] They *sound* like the horsemen. But they are not. In a strange way they are things worth fighting *for*, things you need for your development — as we shall see.

An introduction to the hard life

You may recall that I was teasing out some ideas about war, hunger and other such treasures and indicating that:

1. A Christian has a duty to strive, to 'build the world', one aspect of this being to try to eliminate hunger, and unemployment and pain and war — the physical deprivations man suffers from. Some people channel their action in this regard through politics; most make their contribution through their ordinary work and social intercourse and disposing of surplus income (compulsorily, by taxation, and voluntarily, by investment, loan, gift etc).

2. Each person in his life encounters some pain, certain limitations, which he cannot escape from. They are part of the human condition. In this sense they are God-given and have a positive value, so it would be a bad thing as well as a stupid thing to *try* to escape from them; yet many people insist on trying and are therefore always frustrated.

In other words: we Christians have no quarrel with any man; we have no franchise and no vocation to wage war on the world. And we have no quarrel with God — no right to try to shed our human limitations.

Yet despite all this, in the same breath I was sending you best wishes, wishing you *would* experience hunger and pain and loneliness and death, implying that they were good things. Let me explain what I mean. And remember it's not my aim to play with words, that's not the game I'm in, nor one I'm recommending.

Yet there is a war, a good war; there *is* a quarrel you have to pick. As St Paul put it in one of his more high-flown passages: 'It is not against human enemies we have to struggle, but against the Sovereignties and the Powers who originate the darkness in this world, the spiritual army of evil in the heavens.... So stand your ground, with truth buckled round your waist, and integrity for a breastplate, wearing for shoes on your feet the eagerness to spread the gospel of peace and always carrying the shield of faith so that you can use it to put out the burning arrows of the evil one. And then you must accept salvation from God to be your helmet and receive the word of God from the Spirit to use as a sword' (Eph 6:11-12, 14-17).

He also noticed that 'I cannot understand my own behaviour. I fail to carry out the things I want to do, and I find myself doing the very things I hate.... I can see that my body follows a different law that battles against the law which my reason dictates.' The way out of this, he says, is through grace, which will allow you to 'make every part of your body into a weapon fighting on the side of God' (Rom 7:15, 23; 6:13).

How are you and I to win this war, to achieve peace? It 'is accessible only to men of good will, for it is the inheritance only of those who win it by fighting their own selfishness and the bad tendencies we all carry within us and which want to be satisfied at all costs.... You, are you fighting? You know that I'm not talking about armed conflict between states, about bombing by urban guerillas or revolutionary or anti-revolutionary commandos, or about the more modest struggle to paint walls and hoardings with noisy denunciations, to show your protest or your support and, incidentally, to annoy your neighbours. I'm talking about something much more difficult: I mean cutting the heads off that monstrous Hydra of your selfishness; fighting your impurity and lies and hypocrisy (first our own and if before we die we win that battle then maybe we can do something about other people's) and laziness and frivolity and foolish pride, and complaining and bourgeois attitudes to life: the whole shooting gallery'[15]

In other words, if you are to develop as a person and a Christian you must in a sense create your own pain. The logic is that if you don't do this you will become, say in ten or twenty years, a sort of accident. You will be the result of coping with a series of things which have happened to you, instead of being an achievement, the result of plans pursued.

Friend: if you want to live, you must die to yourself. If you want even to avoid losing ground, you must swim against the tide.

A QUIET LIFE?

It's all terribly earnest, isn't it? All I want is a quiet life, a decent life. I don't want to harm anyone. Live and let live, tolerance, calm: are these not values to prize? Maybe; but the way to lay hold of them is by striving. What right have you, or I, to a quiet life as long as just one other man, woman or child has no such ease? Christ was the arch-radical: he was so much at odds with evil, sin and deprivation that he emptied himself and became the Man of Sorrows, offering his life in order to liberate all other lives. If we as Christians, as men and women, feel for the condition of others, the way to alleviate that condition is not by words, bombs and violence against establishments but by rebelling against ourselves. If we in our heart of hearts want to be Christ-like we have to realise that 'anyone who does not take up his cross and follow in my footsteps is not worthy of me.... Do not suppose that I have come to bring peace to the earth: it is not peace I have come to bring but a sword' (Mt 10:38, 34).

52 An introduction to the hard life

If those who labour and are overburdened approach Jesus he will give them rest. They have to shoulder his yoke and learn from him, but it is an easy yoke and his burden is light (cf. Mt 11:28-30). Fine: if you are overburdened there is a straight way to that good ease. But *you* are not overburdened; you are the picture of health; you are in the top one per cent of the world; yours is the easy life. *You* have to pick a quarrel.

You are no waif; I don't see you as a wino, hung up on drugs, emaciated, cancerous, homeless. You, friend, and I are westerners, living in a welfare state, properly fed, surrounded by toys, with holidays every year (every six months?, every weekend?), with neat bodies and relatively clean souls, educated, dressed, motorised, menued, secure. All these facilities, *all these good things*, all these riches are just so many obstacles: it is easier for a camel to pass through the eye of a needle than for us to enter the kingdom of God. When Christ said that shocking thing his listeners asked, 'In that case, who can be saved?' (they were very bright: they knew that *they* were rich), and he replied, 'Things that are impossible for men are possible for God' (cf. Lk 18:24-27). Well, God will show you the trick and help you use it. In fact, if you read the Gospels you will find lots of tricks, all sorts of commandments, hints and advice and cajolings.

Don't let me exaggerate: it's not only for the twentieth-century bourgeois that this 'self-starting' striving Christianity comes into its own. It is in one way or another the staple diet of every man or woman who has died in God's friendship.

'But doesn't all this insistence on struggle' (Monsignor Escrivá[16] was asked a few years ago) 'make the Christian vocation inaccessible to people?' 'It doesn't make it in accessible', he replied, 'it makes it real. We all know it. We experience something dragging us down. St Augustine used to say his clothes were being tugged by his bad passions — in other words, those things which we are ashamed of if we consent to them, vile things, things which do not suit a son or daughter of God. And alongside that our heart holds many desires to do great things, to make immense sacrifices: clean, noble, wonderful ambitions to do good. For God's help lifts us up and fills us with ideals and cleanliness: that's the action of the Holy Spirit in your soul. We have to learn to do good, *discite benefacere*, and to say "No" to him who drags us down, the devil.

'God's grace tells us to be good, to be faithful, to be loyal, to sacrifice ourselves, to be cheerful, to give good example, to overcome ourselves more often, not to yield where we ought not yield. Our passions tell us the opposite. The battle is set up. Each one of us knows that in things of this sort, which are constants in our life, we are in two minds. We hesitate because we are free, because we can do either the good thing or the bad thing. If we do the good thing with God's grace, it is a victory; if we do the bad thing, it is a defeat.'

But can struggle of this sort really bring joy?

'Of course. Struggle creates and conserves joy. All of you — from the youngest to those of us who are not so young — have experienced the joy brought about by this struggle in our soul: a struggle known only to God and ourselves; and, in confession, to the priest to whom we open our soul. We have to fight every day; every day we have to try to win — and many times every day. True, we try to join battle far from the main walls of our fortress: for in this way, if we do not win the damage is not very important;[17] we feel very ashamed when defeat comes we return to God with an athlete's resilience. It is St Paul, not I, who speaks about this spiritual athletics, this sport'.

IT'S A GAME

Fighting and dying and war do not turn you on? Forget them. You see: it's not a war, it's a game: it has slipped, flipped neatly from war to game. What St Paul said was: 'All the runners at the stadium are trying to win, but only one of them gets the prize. You must run the same way, meaning to win. All the fighters at the games go into strict training; they do this just to win a wreath that will wither away, but we do it for a wreath that will never wither. That is how I run, intent on winning; that is how I fight, not beating the air. I treat my body hard and make it obey me, for, having been an announcer myself, I should not want to be disqualified' (1 Cor 9:24-27). Being a Christian involves you in a sort of athletics: you train and diet and try and lose and try and win and lose and win and win. So it's not so much a matter of having nice sentiments or feeling good or going around praising the Lord. It's a more businesslike affair. You have to learn it. It's rarely dramatic — like when you really win; it's much more typically a matter of little things, a certain doggedness, getting used to saying 'No' to yourself.

Monsignor Escrivá really pursued that simile. You perhaps know the point in *The Way* which goes: 'You tell me: when the chance comes to do something big, then! ... Then? Are you seriously trying to convince me — and to convince yourself — that you will be able to win in the supernatural Olympics without daily preparation, without training?'[18] Around the time of the Olympics, in a conversation with a PE instructor, he recalled: 'I saw how those strong fellows with their poles would come up to jump. They concentrated in silence until — at last! — it looked as though they decided to go. But no, a fly had buzzed past and broken their concentration. They were much more recollected than many Christians are when it's time for prayer.

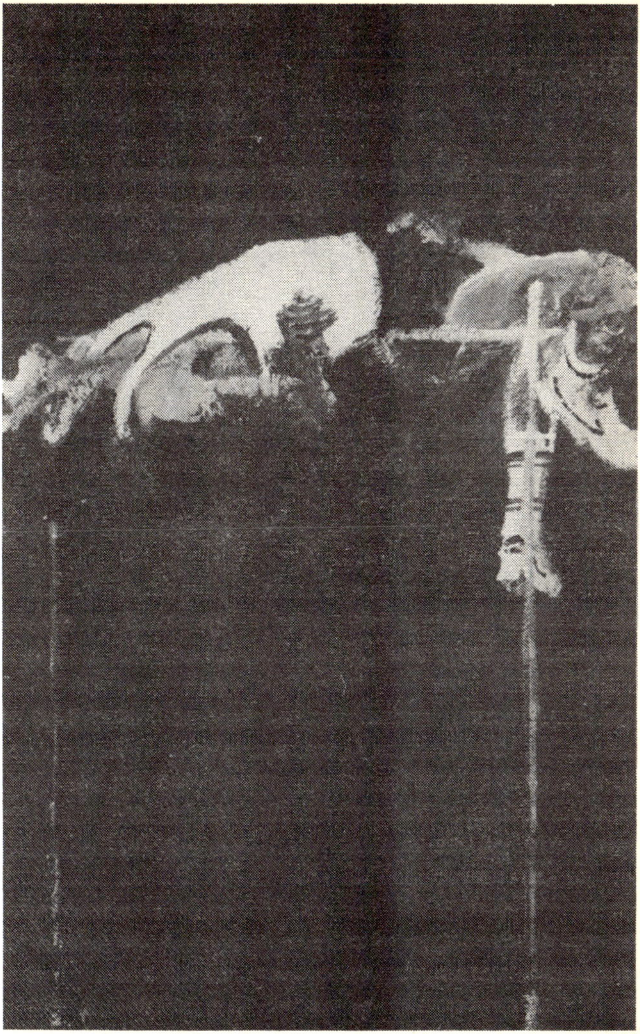

'At other times they didn't stop; they wanted to jump but ... they couldn't. Then they hung their head, made their way back to the start, limbered up and again got into that state of physiological recollection, which must have been psychological recollection at the same time. Then on they came and, perhaps at the fourth or fifth try, they jumped.

'You should tell your students that the same thing happens in life. Tell them that they are not animals; that in these times of violence, of brutal, savage sexuality, they have to be rebels. You and I are rebels: we don't want to be animals. We want to relate to God and we try to fulfil those spiritual practices which go with our vocation. To do this it is helpful to know how to do supernatural gymnastics: they are very similar to — or at least parallel to — physical gymnastics.... To help us jump successfully you and I have God's grace and the protection of our Lady. So, '*We can do it!*' we will say with those poor Apostles who were so daring; they did not yet know that in order to be able to do it (drink Christ's "chalice") they had to experience the Cross. We do know it. And with God's grace and that of our Lady, I repeat, *we can do it!* but only by fighting. He who does not fight is a coward'.

Because a person's body can get sick, broken or old, every athlete's career must come to an end and from then on he must be content with keeping fit. In the spiritual life it's not quite the same: you can always improve, you can always grow: by keeping up your exercises and setting yourself goals you will find you *can* overcome. And in particular you will find that you can grow in the main qualities the Christian religion brings — the special theological virtues of faith, hope and charity: these really identify you with God and you can obtain them only by God's gift. But although he has a perfect right to be random in his allocation of gifts he does tend to take note of our effort. There is a lyric in *My Fair Lady* where Eliza Doolittle challenges her wooer: 'Words, words, words! If you're in love, show me!' I don't suppose the lyric writer knew that St John had got there before him: 'My children, our love is not to be just words or mere talk, but something real and active' (1 Jn 3:18). So your effort to be a better person is rewarded by God who makes you a better god. Don't be shocked, let me explain.

THREE THINGS

The absolutely essential means which a Catholic must use to become what God wants him to be are: prayer, and mortification or self-denial, and the sacraments.

If you don't pray, or deny yourself or go to the sacraments, you are asking for trouble. If you do pray, do deny yourself and do go to confession and Eucharist regularly, you 'will see, in undreamt-of colour and relief, the wonders of a better world, of a new world: and you will draw close to God . . . and know your weakness . . . and be deified . . . with a deification which, by bringing you nearer to your Father, will make you more a brother of your fellowmen'.[19]

Now, spiritual athletics is precisely your effort to:

1. overcome your mental laziness and pray, especially by liturgical prayer (the Mass), mental prayer (time you take out to pray) and prayer-at-all-times when you make God the focus of your stream of consciousness. None of this will happen *unless you make an effort*;

2. receive the sacraments: not in a routine way but fervently, putting your heart and soul into it: *by making an effort*; and

3. deny yourself — a very uncongenial exercise, you would think. Well, this particularly is the stadium event. And it affects everything we do. Don't think of mortification

as some queer dramatic gesture like standing up to your waist in an icy lake for the love of God (it has been done, and I'm sure God won't reject it: but let someone else do that). Our athletics lie mainly in the area of acquiring human qualities, i.e. becoming a more accomplished, skilled, efficient, agreeable, gentle person. To become better in any way you have to say 'Yes!' to betterness and 'No!' to worseness and to standing still.

Is it time to get up? *Get up.*
Is it time to work? *Work, study.*
Is that book, that magazine, ... an embarrassment? *Close it.*
Is that fellow a bore? *Listen to him.*
Does someone have to put the garbage out? *Why don't you do it?*
Does that friend of yours need to be told something? *Take him aside.*

Some of these things won't take a feather out of you. That simply means that you already have, thank God, some well-developed qualities, 'good habits' which you can retain provided you keep practising them. But others may seem almost unachievable, because *you are defective*. Well, don't just 'say: "That's the way I'm made ... it's my character". It's your lack of character: be a man.'[20] Realise that your effort to work hard, to earn your living, to get your exams (even if 'the system' is a bore), to 'build the world', to hold your tongue, to speak out, to conform to certain conventions which help make life more agreeable to other people: all this effort is not alien or separate from your Christianity: it should be the bread and butter of your Christian living, if you do it for the love of God. 'How afraid people are of atonement! If all that they do for appearance's sake, to please the world, were done with purified intention ... what saints many would be!'[21]

And shall I tell you one area of self-denial which is vital? It is — friendship brought to its logical conclusion, sharing not just our beer or our time or our minds or our bodies but our souls: a Christian must speak to his or her friends about God. (It is self-denial because we are slow to risk ourselves, so concerned about what people will think.) I'm not talking about preaching or lecturing or writing books. You are a temple of the Holy Spirit; through baptism and confirmation you are an apostle. 'When you carry out your "apostolate of discretion and friendship", do not tell me you don't know what to say. For, with the psalmist, I will remind you: "The Lord places on his apostles' lips words filled with efficacy." '[22] Your footgear (remember?) must be, 'eagerness to spread the gospel of peace', and the word of God is your sword: basic equipment.

So, to develop as a Catholic, to be a good Christian, we have to do *all* these three things; you must work your body, and your mind, and your soul. If you were to pray and deny yourself but not receive the sacraments, you would be a good pagan, no matter how much Jesus was on your lips and the bible in your hand.

If you were to pray and receive the sacraments and not deny yourself you would probably be a nice example of the heresy of quietism; and a source of scandal to Christians and non-Christians alike.

If you were to receive the sacraments and mortify yourself and not pray you would be spiritually dead, in the power of the dumb devil.

All these three are ways to become like God — that is the positive aspect, the main aim. But they have a negative aim which must be mentioned (I don't want to slide over it). 'I don't want to put you off and yet I can't treat you as little children who have to have disagreeable truths hidden from them. The *mysterium iniquitatis*, sin, is something very real and very serious. So much so that if committing just one sin could avoid a war (with all the suffering it would bring to innocent people), if one single sin could dispel hunger and thirst, and pain and physical death, it would still be wrong to commit it. Sin is worse than all the evils which it causes. And hunger and thirst and pain and war and death and suffering are just some of the fruits of a first sin, which have been multiplied and increased by all that have come after it.'[23]

YOU CAN'T WIN THEM ALL

Although it's a sport and you should take it seriously, it's also — if I could put it like this — only a sport, a game, and you should not take it too seriously. Don't misunderstand me. What I mean is that being a Christian is not a stoical sort of exercise; biting your tongue, teeth clenched; determined not to sin. Yes, you must strive, but you mustn't put your faith in your own determination. You should try to do everything with good humour and when you fail you should react with sorrow — and humour. A French novelist of the fifties, Camus, an agnostic I suppose, found life absurd, meaningless. He was wrong; and yet there is an element of absurdity in our situation when little men try to be gods, without God: or even when we just try to be men, without God's help: we're forgetful, and proud.

So, if you set yourself up as an adult, relying on determination and good resolution, you do run the risk of being slightly ridiculous in God's eyes; but if you see him as your Father and are humble enough to approach him as a child, he will be charmed even by your clumsiness, your falls.

Remember that a Christian is not a freak. We are not neurotic because in our better moments we want to follow God: it is the most natural thing in the world. A Christian

You can't win them all 61

is a man, a woman, choc-a-bloc with defects. We are capable of all kinds of baseness: every day, as long as we live. 'Don't forget that you are a . . . dustbin. That's why if by any chance the divine Gardener lays his hand on you, and scrubs and cleans you, and fills you with magnificent flowers, neither the scent nor the colour that embellish your ugliness should make you proud. Humble yourself: don't you know that you are a rubbish bin?'[24] You, sir, you, miss, even when you win a race, are doing it on borrowed energies. Don't rest on your laurels: they don't belong to you, and, besides, there's another event just starting.

Won't you join the next race, It is the noblest thing you can do. I would even run a little slower, to help you win. But we can all win, because really it's ourselves we are running against.

Here and now

I was tempted to call this chapter, 'Existentialism and materialism in Christianity' but I was afraid you'd go no further than the title. Yet that's what it is about. 'Now' is the existentialism that realises that the only experience, the only time, we can do anything about is the present one. 'Here' is the materialism of realising that the only situation which matters is that of concrete space — the setting you find yourself in now, this very moment. So if you think it's a good idea to read this chapter ('do what you should be doing'), you can be better for the next few minutes by reading it avidly ('concentrate on what you are doing'): doing those things is the way to become a saint.[25]

We are talking about Here and Now: a situation which is (1) totally transitory and (2) totally real. And I'm going to recommend to you that you concern yourself only with Here and Now if you want to be a better Christian. In a sense I'll suggest that being a good Catholic calls for being an existentialist and a materialist. But I'm not proposing you should follow the philosophical fashions of the day; I would like you to do the thing Christian humanists have always done: appreciate the values of the world *and* see through them.

THE KINGDOM OF HEAVEN YIELDS TO THE VIOLENT

You want to *be*, really to be, to get the most out of life, to *squeeze* it dry? Fine. You want no pie in the sky; you want to have your feet planted firmly on the ground? Fine. That identifies you as a grasper, a man, a woman, who faces reality, a realist. And it marks you as different from the escapist, the dreamer.

Does it 'take all kinds to make the world'? I don't think so. I think that people who opt for a casual, nice, willowy existence do *not* make the world; they unmake it; what happens as a result of their uncommitted casualness is an accident; they are destroyers. Of course, if they purposely and conscientiously develop a coherent lifestyle which is at odds with the accepted norms they are not messers — they may be the forgers of a new society, they may indeed be achievers. But the people who look for an easy way out, an escape: these are losers, later if not sooner.

Only one kind makes the world: the doers, the committers, those whose lives are a *continuous succession of free choices*. Only the existentialists, only the materialists, make the world; and only Christians can really succeed in this making. Have you not heard that the kingdom of heaven has to be taken by storm? (cf. Lk 16:16).

Do you want to *do* something? Let me try to show you that this gut concern does not push your religion aside. On the contrary.

THE TIME IS NOW

In everyone's life the important thing to be is *realistic*, and the important time to be realistic is *now*: a very simple idea, which C.S. Lewis teased out very well in his book of letters from a senior devil to a junior apprentice devil, letters about the tricks to use to tempt humans away from the 'Enemy' (God). Here is how he puts it:

'The humans live in time but our Enemy destines them to eternity. He therefore, I believe, wants them to attend chiefly to two things, to eternity itself, and to that point of time which they call the Present. For the Present is the point at which time touches eternity. Of the present moment, and of it only, humans have an experience analogous to the experience which our Enemy has of reality as a whole; in it alone freedom and actuality are offered them. He would therefore have them continually concerned either with eternity (which means being concerned with Him) or with the Present — either meditating on their eternal union with, or separation from, Himself, or else obeying the present voice of conscience, bearing the present cross, receiving the present grace, giving thanks for the present pleasure.

'Our business is to get them away from the eternal, and from the Present. With this in view, we sometimes tempt a human (say a widow or a scholar) to live in the Past. But this is of limited value, for they have some real knowledge of the past and it has a determinate nature and, to that extent, resembles eternity. It is far better to make them live in the Future. Biological necessity makes all their passions point in that direction already, so that thought about the Future inflames hope and fear. Also, it is unknown to them, so that in making them think about it we make them think of unrealities. In a word, the Future is, of all things, the thing *least like* eternity. It is the most completely temporal part of time — for the Past is frozen and no longer flows, and the Present is all lit up with eternal rays. Hence the encouragement we have given to all those schemes of thought such as Creative Evolution, Scientific Humanism, or Communism, which fix men's affections on the Future, on the very core of temporality. Hence nearly all vices are rooted in the future. Gratitude looks to the past and love to the present; fear, avarice, lust and ambition look ahead. Do not think lust an exception. When the present pleasure arrives, the sin (which alone interests us) is already over. The pleasure is just the part of the process which we regret and would exclude if we could do so without losing the sin; it is the part contributed by the Enemy, and therefore experienced in a Present. The sin, which is our contribution, looked forward...'.[26]

It does make sense. Agree with me: it does make sense. It is too true. It makes irrefutable Christian sense. Have you not heard Christ say: 'That is why I am telling you not to worry about your life and what you are to eat, nor about your body and how you are to clothe it. Surely life means more than food, and the body more than clothing! Look at the birds in the sky. They do not sow or reap or gather into barns; yet your heavenly Father feeds them. Are you not worth much more than they are? Can any of you, for all his worrying, add one single cubit to his span of life? And why worry about clothing? Think of the flowers growing in the fields; they never have to work or spin; yet I assure you that not even Solomon in all his regalia was robed like one of these. Now if that is how God clothes the grass in the field which is there today and thrown into the furnace tomorrow, will he not much more look after you, you men of little faith? So, do not worry; do not say, ''What are we to eat? What are we to drink? How are we to be clothed?'' It is the pagans who set their hearts on all these things. Your heavenly Father knows you need them all. Set your hearts on his kingdom first, and on his righteousness, and all these other things will be given you as well. So do not worry about tomorrow: tomorrow will take care of itself. Each day has enough trouble of its own' (Mt 6:25-34).

Or, consider the nowness of that merchant looking for fine pearls: 'When he finds one of great value he goes and sells everything he owns and buys it' (Mt 13:45-46).

Or St Paul: 'We beg you once again not to neglect the grace of God you have received. For he says: ''At the favourable time, I have listened to you; on the day of salvation I came to your help''. Well, now is the favourable time; this is the day of salvation' (2 Cor 6:1-2).

A SENSE OF URGENCY

Why are Christ and Christians so urgent? Why can't they cool it? Why not wait; didn't he who made time make plenty of it? Isn't tomorrow another day.?

Yet even the pagans are urgent: eat, drink and be merry; tomorrow you'll be dead. But that great storer, that capitalist, planning day after day of secure pleasure, was told: 'Fool. This very night the demand will be made for your soul'. The pagan existentialism bent on security is in fact radically insecure: it is so insecure that it should logically lead to a kind of neurosis. But the Christian existentialism stresses the great value today has for one's eternity — the *lasting* value of transcendence.

Is this Christian urgency a negative thing, a hot-gospelling, rousing appeal to commit oneself to the Lord, in order to ensure your salvation, to escape the jaws of hell; is it tailormade for some Sunday morning TV show? Yes, however inelegant that appeal may seem, however unbecoming, however orientated to one's selfish base instinct of self-preservation: yes, this Christian stress on the urgent need to catch hold of God, to say 'yes' to God, to surrender one's cramped self to God: that is a negative thing — but only in a very superficial sense.

Everything has its negative side. But Christianity is essentially positive. Christ and the Christians are urgent also because they want you to find God, to love God *now*. It would be funny if men were put on earth on trial, on test, as wayfarers, as pilgrims, and yet were expected to spend their lives in strife and noise and confusion and darkness and merely to survive by some grace and go through death in fear and trembling. No: during our life with its ups and downs we are meant to get steadily nearer God, not to grope in circles, in a kind of Blind Man's Buff.

Why are all the saints so urgent?: because they know that God is always there, is always available, is always

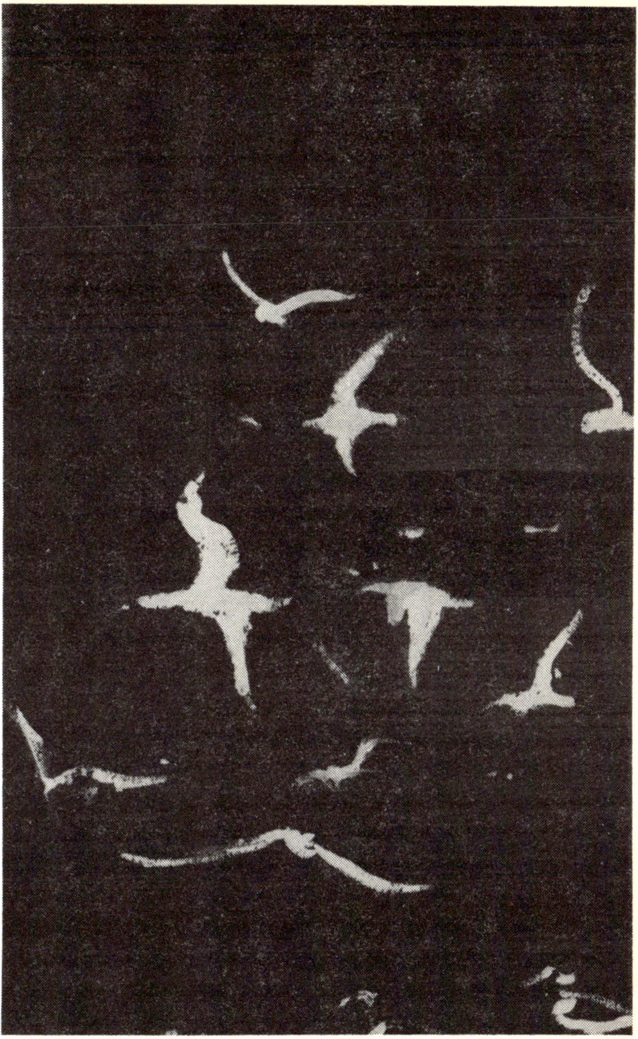

merciful and loves us more than we can ever love him; and because they have experienced him when *they* chose to be there, to be available, to seek his mercy, to love him rather than love themselves. In a word: they found that *it worked*. They speak from experience and when they address us, when they are encouraging us on this subject, they are also urging themselves on. For even if they reached the seventh heaven, that was *yesterday*; it's over, and for today today's troubles are enough. They, like you or me, must be doers if they are to grasp the only reality open to them — the present moment, when God, who is transcendental, can be caught. The key to any Christian's success is the key to anyone's success. This explains the advice St Teresa of Avila gave her nuns: 'Strive like strong men until you die in the attempt, for you are here for nothing else than to strive.'[27]

THE BURDEN OF THE FUTURE

Two other small ideas on this. One is quite repetitive of the ideas above but it has the advantage of being 'pop'. In a Hollywood film I once saw, the boy was proposing but the girl said, 'Not for the time being', to which she received the nice riposte: 'The time being is the only time there is' . . . .

The other comes from a book called *Jesus as friend* in which the author points out,[28] in relation to a person's fear of commitment (to marriage or some other vocation) that 'since these dangers which you imagine possible are not actual dangers and this fear you have has not been verified, then clearly you don't have *yet* the grace of God necessary to overcome them, to accept them. . .'. Shed, therefore, that paralysing fear of the future. I remember noticing a fellow aged, say, twenty five, on the commuter train and thinking: 'Imagine, that poor guy, he's maybe going to spend the next forty years taking this train, day in, day out. It is enough to drive anyone crazy'. It is. It is. And we are most of us very patterned and programmed people (though it's no twentieth-century plot that makes us so). The idea of having to eat breakfast and maybe the same sort of breakfast every morning for the next ten thousand mornings: don't think about it. So, don't try to make the present carry the future: commit yourself to the present and there will be no such thing as a future to frighten you.

Maybe now you can listen to the saying: 'It is not because things are impossible that we do not dare: it is because we do not dare that things are impossible': what panaromas this could open for your ambition!

Kierkegaard explained existentialism in terms of a leap into the dark — with God there to catch you. But the invitation to pursue God rarely calls for a great leap of faith. God knows he is an acquired taste and he expects you to approach him gingerly. But, do taste him. You will find that he is sweet.

CHRISTIAN MATERIALISM

But *where* are you to find him? Where is the Christian *place*? Listen to another master, a great doer. In the course of a Mass on the campus of Navarre University Monsignor Escrivá said the following. I know it's a long quotation; but here it is, accessible to you, from what I regard as one of the *great* sermons:

'. . . everyday life is the true setting of your lives as Christians. . . . You must realise now — more clearly than ever — that God is calling you to serve him *in and from* the secular and civil activities of human life. He waits for us everyday, in the laboratory, in the operating theatre, in the army barracks, in the university chair, in the factory, in the workshop, in the fields, in the home and throughout the whole panorama of work. Be sure of this: there is "something" holy, something divine, hidden in the most ordinary situations, and it is up to each one of you to discover it. . . .

'There is no other way. Either we learn to find our Lord in ordinary, everyday life, or we shall never find him. That is why I can tell you that our age needs to give back to matter and to the apparently trivial events of life their noble, original meaning. It needs to place them at the service of God's Kingdom, it needs to spiritualise them, turning them into a way and an opportunity for a continuous meeting with Jesus Christ.

'The genuine Christian approach — which professes the resurrection of the body — has always quite logically opposed "dis-incarnation", without fear of being judged materialistic. We can, therefore, rightly speak of a "Christian materialism", which is boldly opposed to those materialisms which are blind to the spirit. . . .

'It is understandable that the Apostle should write: "all things are yours, you are Christ's and Christ is God's" (1 Cor 3:22-23). We have here an ascending movement which the Holy Spirit, poured into our hearts, wants to call forth in this world — upwards from the earth to the glory of the Lord. To make it clear that everything is included in that movement, even what seems commonplace. St Paul also wrote: "in eating, in drinking, do everything as for God's glory" (cf. 1 Cor 10:31).

'This doctrine of holy Scripture, as you know, is to be found in the very core of the spirit of Opus Dei. It should lead you to do your work perfectly, to love God and your fellowmen by putting love into the little things of your everyday life and discovering that "divine something" which is hidden in small details. The lines of a Castilian poet are especially appropriate here: "Write slowly and with a careful hand, for doing things well is more important than doing them...".'

'I have just said, live your everyday lives in a holy way. And with these words I refer to the whole programme of your task as Christians. So stop dreaming. Leave behind false idealisms, fantasies, and what I usually call "mystical wishful thinking": If only I hadn't married, If only I had a different job or qualification, If only I had better health, If only I were younger, If only I were older.... Instead, stick to real life, the life of here and now: that is where our Lord is: "Look at my hands and my feet," said the risen Jesus, "be assured that it is myself; touch me and see; a spirit has not flesh and bones, as you see I have" (Lk 24:39).

'Light is shed upon many aspects of the world in which you live, when you start from these truths. Take your activity as citizens, for instance. A man who knows that the world, and not just the church, is the place where he finds Christ, loves that world. He endeavours to become properly trained, intellectually and professionally. He makes up his own mind, in full freedom, about the problems of the environment in which he moves, and he takes his own decisions in consequence. As the decisions of a Christian, they derive from personal reflection, which strives in all humility to grasp the will of God in both the unimportant and the important events of one's life.'[29]

I know that God can interfere in the very shape of a person's life, asking him to *change his place*. He may want you to become a monk. He may want you to follow him in the intimacy of an apostolic celibacy (which would mean veering from the general direction of marriage); you may have a vocation to the priesthood. So, yes, you may have yet to see your particular vocation clearly. But once you do see it, *only commit*. If your Christian time is now, your Christian place is *here*. In fact you, whoever you are, in ninety-nine cases out of a hundred, can be told now, with my eyes shut, that your place *today* is there where you are.

And yet everyone wants to be somewhere else — with that mystical wishful thinking. And everyone wants *you* to be somewhere else. Turn on the television: they want you to be eating *their* bread, driving *their* cars, in Acapulco, or sipping Vermouth in some disco, or smelling like some perfume factory, or pushing your sex appeal. Your wife wants you to be earning more, your friends want you to come out for a drink. You know, I can almost convince myself that I'm the only one who is not trying to take you out of your place, I who am all urgency: could it be that I am the only one who is not trying to push you around? Could it not be that Christ is the only person who respects you, who loves you as you are?

WHAT ABOUT THE CHURCH?

Despite all his emphasis on the world, on finding God in the ordinary things, on encountering him *now*, don't think that Monsignor Esrivá is promoting a man-centred religion, an activistic religion committed to the world. For a Christian there can be no such thing. A Catholic — and only a Catholic — has access to all the ordinary means to salvation established by Christ and entrusted to the Church. Christ established a visible society — the Church — to last for all time, to pass on the authentic Word of salvation and revelation, and to convey the grace of God through sacraments administered through a hierarchical structure. (A democratic Church? If you want to bring such political terms into play I'm afraid it's much more monarchical and certainly elitist. . . .) All this stuff about the methodology of being a Christian — the practical theology of prayer, joy, self-denial — would be wide of the mark, if it did not presume the essential role of the Church, the priesthood, the sacraments: this role is essential; it is not a matter of paraphernalia and trimmings.

This is the Church you confess in the Creed. And you can if you like say, as many good people have said, 'I believe ... in spite of everything ... in spite of my infidelities. In spite of disarray.'

However, even those rites, even the sacrifice of the Mass, are blunted in their practical effectiveness if you and I do not strive, and do, and seek: we need to exercise the muscles of our souls — however reluctantly, no matter how lethargically.

Don't think that you will become a better person when you are older. True, you are in good company if you think like that. St Augustine — who'd been around — describes himself as being like someone who is trying to wake up but then sinks back into sleep. He knew that God's word was true, but he replied to God's invitation 'with the drowsy words of an idler: "Soon", "Presently", "Let me wait a little longer". But "soon" was not soon and "a little longer" grew much longer'.[30] Do you think that you will solve your problems of purity by getting married? Do not think that some magic will turn irresponsible you into a pillar of household strength. The time to be pure is now, the place for responsibility is here where you are.

And yet why is it that so few people pursue God relentlessly? It's all so simple really, isn't it? It's all in a way so clear, so logical, so reasonable, once you confess belief in Christ as God. Maybe, but we are not logical people, we are unpredictable mixed-up defectivities. And the people who do pursue God, the graspers, the doers, the lovers: what queer breed of men and women are they, what freaks? No, they share our condition, they are made of the same clay. But their secret is that they admit it, they confess it, they glory in their defectivities, in their infirmities. They are humble people, simple people; that is why they strive to abandon themselves into God's hands.

However, in practice people get additional help if they pursue God. Reason and the truths of faith are not the only things that keeps them going. In her *Life* St Teresa tells us that 'a man is unlikely to desire the disapproval and abhorrence of all, or the other great virtues possessed by the perfect, unless he have some earnest of the love which God bears him and also a living faith. For our nature is so dead that *we pursue what we see before us* [my italics] and so it is these very favours [consolations which God gives a soul] which awaken and strengthen faith. But it may well be that I am judging others by my wicked self, and that there may be some who need no more than the truths of Faith to enable them to perform works of great perfection, whereas I, wretched woman, have need for everything'.[31] You see, God rewards his friends *now*.

But to round this off, to come back to earth, to really hit you with that existentialist, materialist Christianity, let's leave aside all the sweeping theory: let me put to you a question which you might kindly put to me: Could you not, would you not, fight a little more — today, there where you are? — to become more like Jesus, so that his Father can recognise you more easily?

The catholic standard

You don't have to go to the Second Vatican Council to learn that *every* Christian is called to be a saint: it's spelt out by Christ, written in the Gospel. But if you think like a *Catholic* you read the Gospel 'in the Church'; you know that the Gospel alone, cut off from tradition, independent of the Church's teaching authority, is open to misinterpretation: you know that the voice of Christ is the voice of the Church.

The Church — and only the catholic Church — teaches the authentic Word of God, through the Bible which the Church identifies and explains to us; through her tradition which is consistent throughout history. She teaches through her more or less articulate preachers; she teaches men and women, who are more or less ready to listen. She teaches through her official magisterium, which is held by the Pope and the other bishops in communion with him and their collaborators — men who, being men, may be arrogant or cowardly at times; she teaches us also by the actions of people like Mother Teresa who are not members of the hierarchy; she teaches also through the word and behaviour of the ordinary Christian-in-the-street, through you and me.

The Church — no matter what happens — goes on. Don't therefore ever appeal to a lack of leadership or of encouragement as the reason for not practising your religion; don't be scandalised by the infidelity or frailty of churchmen: if you are not scandalised by your own failures, why should you be scandalised by others? Everyone is made of the same material, be he pope, priest, journalist or student.

The Church is always at hand, always good for grace. She is only incidentally and superficially an *institution* which must be reformed. Rather than she, it is her members, you and I, sinners, who must be reformed. She is *always* a sure way to get to know God and to get to know yourself. So, when you want to see what way to go as a Christian don't look at what the next person is doing: look at what the Church shows you. Consult your conscience and the teaching and pastors of the Church, and your good Christian friends: not the correspondence columns of newspapers; not even your preferences, your inclinations. Consult, I repeat, your *conscience* and the authentic teaching of the Church. Use your responsible freedom.

Christ says: You must be perfect as your heavenly Father is perfect. But is that possible? Isn't the translation wrong? What does the Greek say? Is it not a recommendation, rather than a commandment? Is not perfection a goal for saints? The guy who is a little slow, who works on an assembly line, whose bowels never work quite right, whose conversation is punctuated by four-letter words, whose wife is 'plump', who has turned forty but feels fifty five: that fellow?; who may be a Catholic, who *is* a Catholic, but it not really a 'religious kind of person': that fellow? Yeah: him. And, therefore, you — who have perhaps none of those 'commitments'.

That doctrine has always been in the Church; but the ecclesiastical culture and Christians' lukewarmness obscured it. Vatican II spelt it out: by baptism we receive a calling to be holy: it is our 'duty' to be holy. Don't think that holiness is for a privileged set of people, for a special class: we are all called to holiness.

However, the teaching of the Vatican Council has yet to be put into effect; it has yet to be 'believed'. It will take more time before our pastors clearly and boldly and consistently and encouragingly preach this teaching by their word and example, in season and out of season — before they strive to introduce it into our minds and into our eyes. And it will take us even longer to do anything about it.

MEASURERS

Let's not be afraid. Let's look at a sketch of the Catholic who has not come to terms with this 'universal call to holiness'. He knows the rules; there are the commandments of God (which he sees as prohibitions) and the commandments of the Church. Now the commandments of the Church about 'religious observance' are simple and precise; they are basically: (1) you have to go to confession, if you are conscious of having committed mortal sin; (2) you have to go to Mass on Sundays; (3) you must go to the Eucharist once a year (the Easter duty).

You may think that that's not very much. You are right — and wrong. The best thing in this world is to be in the grace of God. And if you keep those commandments you are his friend.

However, there are other rules which are equally simple but not nearly as precise: Christ tells us, in the Bible, that we must love the Lord our God with our whole heart and our whole mind and our whole strength. And St Paul says in the same book we have to pray always. And Christ says we must take up our cross daily; and that when we pray we should go into our upper room and pray so God can hear us, instead of wanting to be regarded by spectators as 'holy people'.

How do you marry these two lots of commandments? Basically by seeing the first as a *minimum* and the second as a maximum. The Church does not leave you 'free' with regard to the first: there is no discussion about those duties, though of course you are a free agent and any religious observance is useless unless it is exercised in freedom, from the heart. (Also a person may be so uneducated in his faith that he or she is just plain ignorant of what it involves. God will make allowances for someone in that position.)

But with regard to the second lot we have a great freedom of choice. How am I to love God with all my mind? The Church will give me guidance from her experience; and she will try to woo me into loving God; but she goes no further than that. The Church — in her law — addresses all Christians; but in her pastoral action, if I might make that crude distinction, she must address people who differ in character, social position, intellectual capacity, age etc; there is no precise law of religious observance that she can or would impose. None but one: the great liberating law that each Christian should look for *holiness*, there where he is: now, not tomorrow.

The Catholic who does not come to terms with this law has a hard time. *He* is the one who has the hard time. He wants to survive as a Christian: good. I pray that I may do so. But his attitude is all very sombre and negative. His God — who still is God — is a spoil sport; a strict judge; a measurer of merit; a stalking hunter. The great ideal of this man is to avoid serious sin or to avoid having to accuse himself of serious sin. Or if he has committed grievous sin and can't deny it, his purpose is reluctantly to go to confession. He is never really at ease with God or man; everything he does is flavoured with mediocrity: even his enjoyment, no matter how elated he may become, he soon sees as empty because it is *selfish* — it is not shared. Sometimes he does rise by doing things which have the good of others as their primary goal or by engaging in 'social work'; but his relationship with his wife, his child, his friend, the world, is rather shallow and formal. The only *person* to whom he really confesses his purpose is himself; these activities are not shared by God. Why? Because God is a kind of intruder. It is, he admits, God's world in some way or other; but he'd prefer, if it were *his* choice, a world without God: of course, a just world etc., but one where he could do what he liked without this *interference* of conscience.

This man is missing out. He is certainly missing out as far as genuine Christian *joie de vivre* is concerned. And as far as limited pagan *joie de vivre* goes, he hasn't got that either. No wonder he so easily flips into unbelief: put him in a hostile environment, let him get used to being in mortal sin for a few weeks, add a dash of critical spirit and hypocritical anticlericalism: instead of a Catholic we have a lapsed one.

PEDESTRIANS

Let me give you another caricature: the Catholic who wants to be 'good'. He or she is devout: morning and night prayers, perhaps the family rosary, daily Mass even, a sense of the spiritual value of suffering and self-denial; who visits the sick or is in some pious association. Well, *that* person, who is a *contributor* to the Church, who is an asset to the Mystical Body: that person can and often does fall very short of his potential: he has not come to terms with the universal call to holiness — no matter how good he is (much better than our first friend): he still has a long way to go. He is clever enough and humble enough to realise that he could be better, but he doesn't know how to go about it. He would not *mind* being better; he knows that many people are much better than he is; but he has come to terms with his spiritual life; he has reached a kind of plateau. It's higher and feels safer than the first person's; but it is rather flat. He does take up his cross but it is a bit of a drag. He is a pedestrian.

Saints? Now, they are different. They, he thinks, are special people endowed with special gifts and key missions. Saints are born, he'd say, not made. They have native resources which allow them to make whatever effort is necessary to be great. He would never say they are fanatics because he knows fanaticism is a sin and saints are not sinners....

He is wrong. He does not know what holiness is. He has not heard about the *universal* call to holiness. He too is losing out. He has found his level. To use another metaphor: he is a settler, he has settled down: doing good things when he could do better.

TO BE BETTER

But what about the person who knows that he should be a saint and that only *he* can get in the way of his being a saint? If he decides to do something about it, what he is doing is deciding not to be a 'good person' but to be better. It is really a much more accessible goal, and besides it is the goal which Christ puts before us: *to be better*.

Could you not be a little bit better? Yes, I could. No matter where I stand I could be a little better — in this sense: that however unwilling I may be to make the effort, I realise that I could make it if I chose to. Well, *that effort*, that little choice, can change any man's life.

Immediately, he changes from being a pedestrian or a settler or whatever he was to being a child, a soldier, an athlete, a pilgrim, a worker, a doer — a free man.

What is going on? He is taking a leaf out of St James' book: that tough old bishop wrote this to the Jewish Christians throughout the world: 'You must do what the word tells you, and not just listen to it and deceive yourselves. To listen to the word and not obey is like looking at your own features in a mirror and then, after a quick look, going off and immediately forgetting what you looked like. But the man who looks steadily at the perfect law of freedom and makes that his habit — not listening and then forgetting, but actively putting it into practice — will be happy in all that he does' (1:22-25).

Note the reward (it's nothing to be ashamed of): he will be happy in all that he does. Most people spend their time trying to be happy — and are unhappy. Whereas this fellow gets there by another route entirely: he looks *steadily* at the *law* of *freedom, actively* putting it into practice. He is happy in all that he does — not just in his 'religious observances', but in his work, and family life and leisure also.

CONVERSION AND HOLINESS

Stay a little longer. Have you noticed that I haven't talked about 'conversion' or 'opting for Christ' or 'choosing Jesus'? Some people think that being a good Christian involves a dramatic conversion — *Halleluiah*! — when the Spirit of the Lord comes on them or they open themselves to the Lord and all is utterly changed. Be warned. Do not think that is the only way or the best way or the normal way to the spiritual life. It can help to be bowled over provided that you don't rest in that experience — that would mean that holiness was a matter of *attitude* or of an endowment of grace calling for no effort on our part. I confess I am afraid for people who go that way — afraid that one day they may under the pressure of some event wake up and find it was all a dream.

It is good 'to open yourself to the Spirit' — but not by a great cerebral effort of 'faith' or a poetic leap in the dark: that is a recipe for disaster because it's tempting God: faith comes from him, as a gift, and his voice is not in the night-wind or in the earthquake or in the fire but in the whisper of a gentle breeze (cf 1 Kings 19:11-12); and leaps in the dark are dangerous unless God tells you to make them.

To become holy simply requires that you — with your mind and emotions, with your personality such as it is now — look at the law of freedom and actively put it into practice. Holiness is a sort of pilgrim's progress.

It even may mean that you have to go against the grain. In fact we have it on good authority that it does mean that. Christ in his preaching was very matter of fact: he said: 'Repent'. And until we *have* actually said 'I'm sorry' and set about showing we mean business, we cannot even understand the idea of holiness.

So much for spontaneity: it's a sugar, nice if it's there. It's no great exercise of your freedom to do whatever you feel like. But to do the good thing you don't (particularly, at this moment) feel like — that is the way to real Christian joy. It is much more human, more 'manly', to do what has to be done than to pirouette and argue and hum and haw like the measurer. And apart from being more elegant it is *easier*. For the poor fellow who's a minimalist, everything, every little new thing in favour of God, is the result of a Great Debate or is done slowly and grudgingly: but the person who decides to be better — he gets on with the job.

BACK TO SCHOOL

But remember: the person who decides to be better is a learner. He's like a young child who is happy to go off to school in the morning: new day, new class, new battle. The people who think they 'know it all' have nothing else to learn: they are losers, and aged.

If we want to be better and can be better, then we don't 'know it' until we do it, because religion is not knowing the law or the rules: it is living and doing. And since we can always be better, a little better, we are always ready to be encouraged and helped and have our mind jogged. That is why the doer makes himself available to be taught — by the Church through its magisterium, and by 'schools' within the Church which have this very purpose, and by his spiritual guide. He needs a guide. 'Without an architect

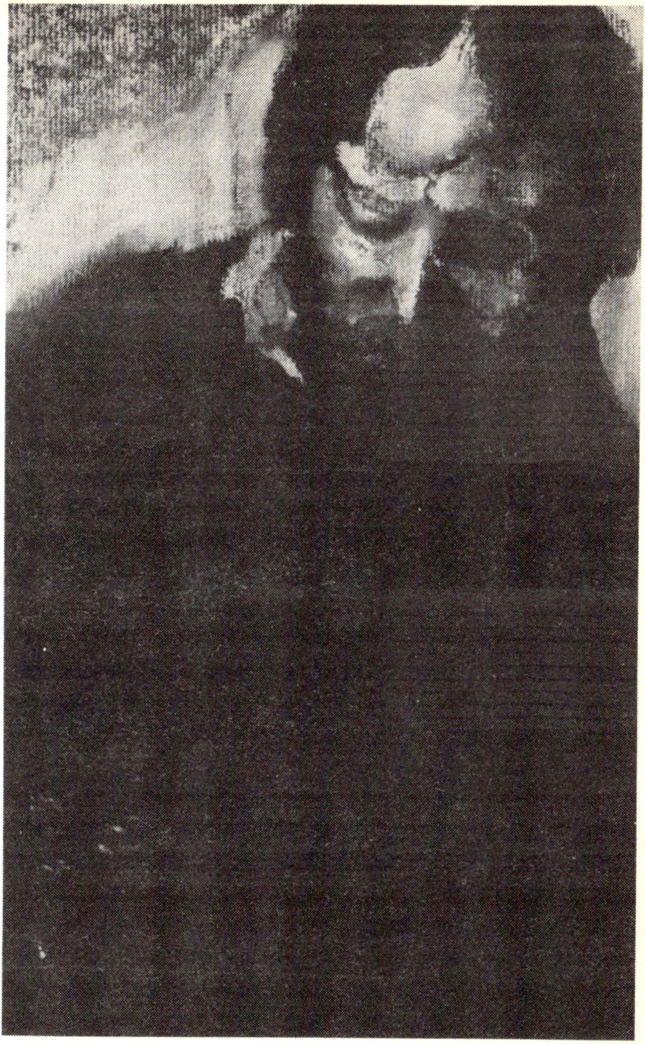

you wouldn't build a good house for your life on earth. How then, without a Director, can you hope to build the palace of your sanctification for your eternity in heaven?'[32] If you are in solitary confinement: don't worry. But otherwise you need a person who will 'second the work of the Holy Spirit in your soul':[33] he won't take away your freedom, his job is to help you build it.

If you don't get this kind of help you are liable, Christian though you be, to feel like some existentialist, lost in a huge anonymous sea of (redeemed) humanity — especially if you are striving to be better. You need periodic encouragement and monitoring if you are to sanctify the routine detail of your existence. Many people will get this help through the sacrament of penance — but it is distinguishable from the sacrament. Try to find it. You are not simply a Christian who can be given a Bible in a plain envelope; you are not simply a member of the 'People of God' who is immersed in a collectivity, a community: you are a man, a woman, for whom Christ has died; you are a baptised *person* and you have a right to and need for *personal* help to mature the grace of baptism and confirmation.

Why not complicate your life? Look for some good adult education, on a subject which really matters: *learn* to be better.

A sense of identity

I would like to take leave of you with two remarks — one about 'sources' and the other about 'identity'.

SOURCES
Although there are huge tracts of shared territory in 'religion for young (or old) Catholics' and 'religion for young (or old) Protestants', there are also areas of substantial difference. One of these has to do with the source of Christian doctrine: the non-Catholic Christian goes to the Bible; the Catholic goes to the Church (where of course he finds that very Bible). If you are to be a mature Catholic, you need to seek the explanation of the faith from the Church. And where must you not look for it? In your experience.

But: don't we learn by experience; isn't that the best way to learn? No, I'm afraid it's not. The very fact that you are reading these lines is proof that you are exposing yourself additionally to other people and to their experiences and views: if you don't think that's sensible you should close this book *immediately*. If you were to rely on your own first-hand experience you could never know Christ and never be a Christian. If you were really to rely on your own experience you would systematically commit every sin in the book 'just to see for myself'. And you would progressively disintegrate as a personality.

To be a good Catholic you must go to the Church; there you will find Christ present — present in the sacraments which make a Christian to be more Christ, and present in the word of God which is authoritatively preached only by the bishops and other clergy. In the Church also you find the Christian heritage — the saints who have gone before and the Communion of Saints generally and the Church's accumulated wisdom. That wisdom belongs to you; in suitable doses, well-prescribed, you should use it to nourish your soul, your interior life — the *Confessions* of St Augustine; the ancient creeds; the decisions of the ecumenical councils; the writings of the Fathers; the theology of St Thomas; the prayer books of the people; the history of the Church; Cardinal Newman. . .: the list is virtually endless.

THE LIGHT OF THE GENTILES

But let me suggest now — because it suits my purpose — that if you ever have to go off to a desert island, a concentration camp, a prison, a new Ethiopia or to some God-forsaken spot, you take with you as well as the Bible, and *War and Peace*, and your fancy, a copy of the Second Vatican Council's Constitution on the Church — it's a document called *Lumen gentium* (the light of humanity) which is the Church trying to explain itself. It is a very Catholic source and though it's quite recent lots more people will have to read it before it's shot its bolt. I'd like you to read it not only because it's about the Church but because it's about *you*.

Elsewhere I've touched on this business of 'holiness'; I took as my cue this same document. It underlines that *all* Christians (and that includes us) are through baptism called to holiness. Holiness is the whole point of religion. However, *in fact* some Christians are more holy than others, for the simple reason that they use their freedom to strive for the fullness of Christian life: these are the people who are availing of the radical equality that exists in the Church. These are the radicals, and Christ invites all to be radicals and revolutionaries in this sense. No one is 'more' than you except by dint of forgetting himself more than you have. And no one who is 'less' than you can be helped by taking some of your 'more' — his own effort and Christ's generosity (O.K. and your *help*) is the only way he can grow as a Christian.

So: the radical equality of Christians. A very sobering notion because it means that none of us can blame the clergy, or the big farmers, or the captitalists, or the workers or the educational system if Christianity 'doesn't seem to work': the first person to be blamed is oneself.

CHRISTIANS ARE NOT ALL EQUAL

But *Lumen gentium* also stresses that from an additional point of view all Christians are *not* equal; because people in the Church have different functions. And basically there are three such roles:

1. the clergy: pope, bishops, priests;
2. religious: members of religious orders;
3. lay people.

To be a good Christian is not a matter 'simply' of 'being a good Christian'; holiness is indeed a function of receiving the sacraments and getting on closer terms with Jesus through prayer, but it is also a matter of 'doing God's will' and that means discovering and following your particular vocation. I don't want here to get involved in the important subject of Vocation. God's will for a person can be very particular; but let me put it broadly: to be a good Christian means also fulfilling your role in the Church. You might almost say that being a good Christian is not so much a matter of doing good (things) as of doing (things) well.

A man who is a priest must primarily become a good Christian, a saint, through being a priest and doing what a priest has to do; a nun, sister, monk, missionary priest, can only pull her or his weight in the Church, can only develop as a Catholic by being good at being a nun, monk etc; and a 'lay person' can only become a saint by doing what a lay person has to do.

Now the curious thing is that whereas the priest has a very 'churchy' role (he is an ecclesiastic, a cleric) and the sister and monk pursue the religious life which is notably different from 'ordinary life' (they wear habits, take special vows, etc. and are in a way distanced from everyday life as reminders that there's more to life than foreign travel, nappies, the hard slog), the Church teaches in *Lumen gentium* that the role of lay people *in the Church* is 'to engage in temporal affairs and direct them according to God's will': in other words the *Christian identity* of the ordinary Christian, the route he must follow if he is to develop as a Christian, is to stay exactly where he is, to get on with his job in the world, to develop his ordinary family and leisure relationships and so forth. To be a good Christian he must be *very ordinary* and *very good* at those ordinary things.

I mentioned vocation a moment ago; true, it is very important that each person find out prayerfully what God wants him to do (this time of commitment is usually in adolescence and early adulthood) and set about doing it. But at any point in time 99.99% of Catholics know quite objectively which of the three 'estates' (of clergy, religious or laity) they belong to. (You'll have noted that I have more or less assumed all along that you're one of the laity, a young Catholic man or woman.) Take it that I'm not addressing the .01%.

Are our problems over? No — that is the point I'm coming to. Despite the identity which just being a Catholic should give; despite the additional and necessary identity which knowing where broadly one fits in the Church should give; there is in the catholic Church nowadays a great crisis of identity — a diabolical one, because it brings darkness for a Christian who should be in the light, it confuses when a Christian should be a source of meaning to others.

Perhaps this crisis is basically due to the fact that you and I do not identify with Christ even though we 'put him on' at baptism, as St Paul says. But that's a permanent affliction of man: with the best will in the world we will always fall short of our ideal. The better a man becomes, it seems, the more conscious is he of his defects; so if Christians aren't striving to become better maybe we don't have to look any further for the causes of the difficulties of the Church.

And yet do look. Look at this curious phenomenon: Catholics — who as we have seen can by and large only be good Catholics by fulfilling their specific roles in the Church — don't seem to like their places. In some instance priests are reluctant to dress as priests — they dress as 'lay men'; having no patience or appetite or faith in their function as preachers and makers of the body and blood of Christ and midwives of the spiritual life in souls (how understandably, because their help is not sought) they want to go off and work alongside the ordinary worker so as to get 'closer to him' and preach that way, running the risk of being seen as sorry freaks. Or they think that they can preach through a sort of gospelly pop groups (that is enough to put goose flesh on any normal Christian). Or, following a mistaken kind of 'liberation theology', they turn religion into politics and acts as if this world were the only life that matters. And it is not me who says it, but the Pope, that many bishops — who should be rulers of God's people, not afraid to tell them hard true sayings — have let themselves be muzzled by the 'democratic' committees which arise nowadays by almost spontaneous generation and seek to tell the bishop what not to preach;

or have settled into mere pastoral busy-ness which lets everyone do his own thing, go his own way, preach his own heresy provided he 'professes' some sort of faith in the Church.

But I don't want to talk about the particular identity problems of the clergy or of religious; that's too easy, it's impertinent, and it's an indulgence because there's not a great deal you and I can do about that other than (1) pray and (2) make sure that *we* know what *we're* at. Let me warn you therefore about a way which lay people might think was their Christian high road but which really is a dead end.

THE 'CHURCHY' CATHOLIC

Being a good Catholic, becoming even a saint, does not mean you have to become a church person — in the sense that you have to be physically around the church building or become a lay minister of the Eucharist or get involved in church ('ecclesiastical') organisations or exercise some sort of democratic right which gives you your say in matters of faith and morals and how the Church is run; nor does it mean that *the* thing to do is read lessons or strum a guitar or sing tidied-up lyrics from rock albums at Mass. No: your Christian identity is found by 'engaging in temporal affairs and directing them according to God's will' — cleaning the street (if that's your job), relaxing with your friends, making friends with your children (if you have any). By doing these things well you develop as a Christian; by neglecting them or giving them little importance, you dry up. You, to the extent that you become 'clerical' or 'religious', have lost *your* Christian identity. Isn't that consoling — that Christ wants only your heart?

FREEDOM AT LARGE

Yes, to engaging in temporal affairs. I'm on. But don't

I have to direct them according to God's will? Does not this mean that I have to keep running back to the churchmen to get advice on moral problems and on how to do apostolate? No, sir.

Vatican II's *The Church in the Modern World*[34] has a lot of clear things to say on this subject. Of course the Church has a lot to say about the morality of many social questions. And you as a lay person have to listen to that teaching and make it yours: it is your task, the Council says, 'to cultivate a properly informed conscience and to impress the divine law on the affairs of the earthly city. For guidance and spiritual strength let them [lay people] turn to the clergy *but* [my emphasis] let them realise that their pastors will not always be so expert as to have a ready answer to every problem (even every grave problem) that arises: this is not the role of the clergy, it is rather up to the laymen to shoulder their responsibilities under the guidance of Christian wisdom and with eager attention to the teaching of the magisterium'. Nice stuff: doesn't it make you feel like a man-in-the-world, a son of God, rather than some appendix of a 'church' consisting largely of indifferent architecture and ecclesiastical officialdom?

Given that — with the essential help of those very bishops and priests — you strive to identify with Christ by prayer and sacrament and the development of virtue, you operate, Christian in the world, as a *free agent*. If you use this freedom well and work hard, with plenty of human ambition, you will do two great things: you will become a saint yourself, and also you will help other people to know Christ, to see Christ, through you as an individual and through the culture you create.

A CHRISTIAN CULTURE

For, don't think that Christianity is a hole-in-the- corner thing; or that in the world today Christians must rest content with creating little ghettoes and sub-cultures where they can be safe from 'the world': the Christians — who are men — can't but do what men do: destroy, or build the world. We are not men and certainly not Christians if we throw in the towel. There is every reason why these generations of this century should create a new Christian culture, a culture for our entry into the third millenium. It's not a matter of bringing back the Middle Ages — cultures are human things and by definition come and go — but neither is it a matter of abandoning the world and just allowing everything happen under a banner of 'pluralism'. In my country — Ireland — 'pluralism' is a fashionable buzz-word which often really means 'Christianity: OUT' — out of public life, out of the Constitution, out of the laws: 'Christian influence, Christian inspiration: OUT: there are citizens who aren't Christians, so the laws should accommodate *them*' — as if Christian influence implied denying people their human rights, whereas a Christian has a first duty in justice to protect the rights of others. 'Pluralism', in that sense, runs clean contrary to the duty of Christians, and indeed of all men insofar as they recognise that duty, to 'impress the divine law on the affairs of the earthly city'. It pooh-poohs the notion that God has any business in the world: society and the State should be 'agnostic' as far as God's commandments are concerned.

But these commandments are really 'instructions for using the machinery': if they are ignored by society (not just by individuals but by individuals in society), then society simply will not work: it will break down.

Interestingly enough, when you analyse it, you find that 'pluralism' in this sense boils down to promotion of 'sexual freedom'; it says the State should convenience people to pursue 'sexual freedom'; the State should be the three monkeys as far as sexual mores are concerned: hear no evil, see no evil, speak no evil. It is as if the State is using sex as a kind of bread and circuses: distract the people, entertain them; meanwhile the State gets away with pilfering a whole gamut of *genuine* personal rights: the right to life (that's what abortion, for example, steals); the right to work (where is it? many people, especially many young people, are *still* asking); the right to a good education (not manipulated); the right to be able to save enough to have a house; the right to marry and raise a family in a healthy environment; the right to have a penny move from one hand to the other without the State saying 'Wait a moment!'; the right to 'impress the divine law on the affairs of the earthly city'.

A Christian culture does not mean a society run by religious policemen bent on preventing or, worse still, catching people committing sins; it is not a society of sour-faced puritans. It is a society which tries to be *genuinely* pluralist — to let people be themselves and express themselves as they wish, *provided* they don't trample on or undermine the rights of others; it never will succeed 100%, which means that it will make mistakes; but it won't set out to make mistakes, which is what in fact happens in societies which are the product of an ideology. If you would like to get a good general idea of what making a Christian society involves, read Vatican II's *The Church in the Modern World*.

The fact is that there is a culture all around you and it is changing all the time, slowly or quickly, for better or worse, for richer or poorer. It is not just happening: people are making it. If it is shaped by marxists, it will become a marxist culture (which has no notion of pluralism); if it is shaped by 'pluralists', tinkerers, God knows what it will look like forty years down the line. If it is shaped by Christians, by Christian doers, it will be a pretty good scene.

Notes

1 J. Escrivá, *The Way*, 6th edition (Dublin 1986). **2** *Lumen gentium* 8. **3** Cormac Burke, *Crisis-Conscience and Authority*, CTS Do 445 (London 1972). **4** Cormac Burke, *Crisis-Conscience and Truth*, CTS Do 446, (London 1972). **5** *Apostolicam actuositatem* 3; Cf. also 6: "the true apostle is on the lookout for opportunities to announce Christ by word, either to unbelievers, to draw them to the faith, or to the faithful, to instruct them, strengthen them, encourage them to a more fervent life.' **6** *Apos. act.* 12. **7** 'In the religious sphere man is still man and God is still God. In this sphere the peak of progress has already been reached. . . . In the spiritual life, there is no new era to come. Everything is there already, in Christ who died and rose again, who lives and stays with us always', J. Escrivá, *Christ is passing by* (Dublin 1985), 104. **8** Paragraph 23. **9** On the Eucharist, see articles by Charles Connolly and Michael Adams in C. Connolly (ed.), *On being Catholics* (Dublin 1983), pp. 10-48. **10** *The Way*, 194. **11** *The Way*, 217. **12** Cf. Vatican Council II, *Gaudium et spes*, 39. **13** *The Way*, 823. **14** Cf. *The Way*, 194 and 717. **15** Federico Suarez, *La paz os dejo* (Madrid 1973), pp. 68-69. **16** The quotations which follow are taken from a get-together during a two month visit to Spain in the Autumn in 1972. **17** Cf. *The Way*, 307. **18** *The Way*, 194. **19** *The Way*, 283. **20** *The Way*, 4. **21** *The Way*, 215. **22** *The Way*, 972. **23** Federico Suarez, *op. cit.*, pp. 88-89. **24** *The Way*, 592. **25** Cf. *The Way*, 815. **26** C.S. Lewis, *The Screwtape Letters*, Chapter XV. **27** *The Way of Perfection*, Chapter XX in E. Allison Peers, *The Complete Works of St Teresa of Jesus*, Vol. II, (London 1972), p. 86 **28** Salvatore Canals, *Jesus as friend*, 3rd edition (Dublin 1986), p. 72. **29** *Conversations with Monsignor Escrivá de Balaguer*, 2nd ed., Shannon 1972, nos. 114- 116. **30** *Confessions* Book VIII, 11. **31** *Op. cit.*, Vol. 1, p. 60. **32** *The Way*, 60. **33** *The Way*, 62. **34** Paragraph 43.

For further reading

The books mentioned below are currently in print and can be obtained through your bookseller or from your library.

Easy reads

S. Canals, *Jesus as friend* (Four Courts Press, Dublin). Short simple but profound articles on aspects of Christian living.

C. Connolly, ed., *On being Catholics* (Lumen Christi Press, Houston). Shows the importance of the Eucharist, the Blessed Virgin and the authority of the Pope.

J. Escrivá, *The Way* (Four Courts Press, Dublin; Scepter Press, New Rochelle, N.Y.). This is a thought-provoking book, helpful for prayer-use.

J. Orlandis, *A Short History of the Catholic Church* (Four Courts Press, Dublin). Traces the main lines of church history concisely and clearly.

Frank Sheed, *A Map of Life* (Sheed & Ward, London and Christian Classics, Westminster, MD). This is a short introduction to the faith.

M. Tynan, *Catechism for Catholics* (Four Courts Press and Christian Classics, Westminster MD). A new short question-and-answer catechism for adults.

Not-so-easy reads

J. Escrivá, *Christ is passing by* and *Friends of God* (Four Courts Press, Dublin; Scepter Press, New Rochelle). Vigorous homilies full of sound Christian advice on the spiritual life.

J. Hardon, *The Catholic Catechism* (Geoffrey Chapman, London).

B. Kelly, *Introduction to Moral Theology* (Four Courts Press, Dublin).

Lawler, Wuerl and others, *The Teaching of Christ* (Veritas, Dublin).

The Navarre Bible: On-going series of Bible commentaries (Four Courts Press, Dublin).

Frank Sheed, *Theology and Sanity* (Sheed Ward, London). This is an explanation of the main Christian doctrines.

L. Trese *The Faith Explained* (Sinagtala Press, Manila; also available from Four Courts Press, Lumen Christi Press and Scepter Press). A good commentary on the Creed.

A. Flannery, OP, ed., *Vatican Council II: The Conciliar and Post Conciliar Documents* (Dominican Publications, Dublin): especially the documents referred to in this book.

Heavier books

Etienne Gilson, *The Unity of Philosophical Experience* (Christian Classics, Westminster, Maryland). This shows how good philosophy can help one understand the Faith.

Flannery O'Connor, *The Letters of Flannery O'Connor*, ed. Fitzgerald (Vintage Books, New York). A useful insight to a Catholic intellectual at work.